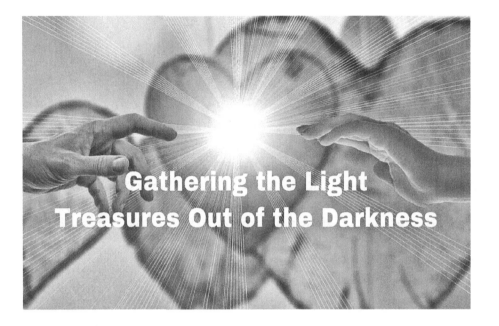

Gathering the Light
Treasures Out of the Darkness

GATHERING THE LIGHT
Treasures Out of the Darkness
by
Sister Anne Marie Walsh, SOLT

Published by Goodbooks Media

Printed in U.S.A.

ISBN: 9798636923152

Imprimatur ✠ R. Walker Nickless, Bishop of Sioux City Diocese, Iowa
5 March 2020

Having reviewed the manuscript entitled *Gathering the Light* by Sister Anne Marie Walsh, SOLT, and with the concurring recommendation of Deacon David A. Lopez, Ph.D., *Censor Deputatus* in this instance, I hereby grant my "*imprimatur*" to this manuscript. Your brother in Christ.
Most Reverend R. Walker Nickless
Bishop of Sioux City

GOODBOOKS MEDIA
3453 Aransas Street
Corpus Christi, Texas 78411
www.goodbooksmedia.com

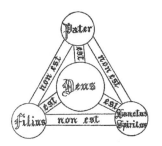

Brothers and sisters:
You were once darkness,
but now you are light in the Lord.
Live as children of light,
for light produces every kind of goodness
and righteousness and truth.
Try to learn what is pleasing to the Lord.
Take no part in the fruitless works of darkness;
rather expose them, for it is shameful even to mention
the things done by them in secret;
but everything exposed by the light becomes visible,
for everything that becomes visible is light.
Therefore, it says:
"Awake, O sleeper,
and arise from the dead,
and Christ will give you light."

Eph 5:8-14

ENDORSEMENTS

Gathering the Light is a beautifully written and timely compilation of short essays and poems. Fully faithful to the Church's vision of reality and redemption, Sr Anne Marie Walsh provides stunning insight into the darkness we discover within us and in the world around us. Though she is not afraid to tackle difficult topics head on, her balance of truth and compassion communicates the tender light of Christ in the most horrific evils in our society. Every entry is worth reading and pondering in depth. Some of my favorites include those on the unique dignity of men and women, and how the disfiguring of God's image in the sexes is manifesting in the most horrific consequences in our lives and culture. I highly recommend this book to anyone who desires to let the light of Christ shine through them, in the midst of darkness.

> **Dr. Bob Schuchts**, nationally renowned speaker,
> author of ***Be Healed*** and founder
> of the John Paul II Healing Center

In *Gathering the Light* Sister Anne Marie rightly points out that each Christian is involved in a war—a civil war against the habits of sin. Only the Power of Grace alone can bring treasures out of that darkness. Sister's reflections speak to the heart of every believer longing for the light that penetrates the darkness of undisciplined desires and brings redemption. Her reflections illustrate the truth that our thoughts become our actions, and our actions become our habits, our habit form our character which determines our destiny. This collection of articles, reflections, and poetry, uses images drawn from our own time to illuminate the beauty of the gift of faith and the light it sheds upon our souls. There is much food for thought in these reflections for each Christian to ponder and draw inspiration from.

Fr. Emmerich Vogt, OP, international speaker, author, and retreat-master, especially known for his teachings on 12-step spirituality and the necessity for self-knowledge, true detachment, and the transforming power of grace that flows from the Cross.

Gathering the Light is an inspiring and rich collection of thought-provoking offerings for the heart, mind and soul. Sr Anne Marie has woven together a beautiful tapestry that has come from the depths of her own ongoing journey with Jesus. This book will invite you to go deeper into your own story, discover the heart of Christ therein and become captivated by the God who loves and heals you.

Sr. Miriam James, SOLT, popular speaker, and author of *Loved As I Am*. Moderator of the popular podcast: *Abiding Together.*

The Light of Christ truly shines throughout Sister Anne Marie's book, *Gathering The Light.* It is a treasure chest of articles and reflections that are easy to read and at the same time guide us to our own inner light.

We all have the light of Christ in us and Sister Anne Marie shows us how to Shine our light in a world that so desperately needs it.

Christine Rossi, Radio Maria Host
of : *A Light in the World*

Sr. Anne Marie lives the charism of Mother Mary, always trusting God in all things. This book gives us a deep reflection into the light of Christ. This pure light, which enlightens our heart, mind and soul, helps us to walk the way of our own cross and guides us through times of darkness. The reflections from this book help us to prepare to live forever in Heaven. By her own unique journey we see the profound relationship Sr. Anne Marie has with Jesus and Mary. As she continues to offer herself completly for the sake of souls, Sr. Anne Marie continues to be a true witness to the love and mercy of God. The Holy Spirit flows through her words!

Sr. Anne Sophie Meaney, foundress of the Society of the Body of Christ and author of: *On the Front Lines, Silent No More, Being Born into Eternal Life,* and *Prayers for the Elderly and All God's Children.*

Gathering the Light is a spiritual treasure for the souls of all who read it, especially for those of us suffering from cancer and severe illness. Sr. Anne Marie Walsh, SOLT, writes from her heart with the pen of God. Her personal stories, her journey with our Lord and her sufferings from cancer inspire us to reach out to Our Heavenly Father and Our Blessed Mother, for what we need, and to seek out His plan for our lives, no matter our circumstances.

I met Sr. Anne Marie when we started *Facing Our Immortality*, a spiritual support group for people and loved ones affected by cancer. She is a gifted writer who loves the Lord with ALL her heart. Her writing is engaging, and every person can see themselves in her stories. Her thought-provoking reflections lovingly facilitate spiritual healing.

Sr. Anne is that gentle spirit, that soothing heart and spiritual guide who will help you understand your life, your suffering and your relationship with God. Her book will help you see your soul, see His love for you and prepare you to fulfill God's dream for your life. We give all Glory to God in thanksgiving for the beautiful works of Sr. Anne Marie.

Denise Archuleta, Co-Founder
of *Facing Our Immortality Ministry*

Table of Contents

Author's Introduction

"...the night is advanced; the day is at hand. Let us then throw off the works of darkness and put on the armor of light...put on the Lord Jesus Christ and make no provision for the desires of the flesh." Rms 13: 11-14

hirty-seven years ago, while I was in the midst of a re-conversion to my faith, I had a dream. I was in a military camp in Roman times. Jesus came over to me, looked at me very firmly, and said: "Take my Armor to the enemy."

I immediately set off to fulfill His command, happy to do whatever He asked but somewhat troubled by his sternness. On the way to the enemy camp, I began to doubt that this command could be right. Would I be leaving Jesus defenseless by taking his armor, his protection away from Him? Was I missing the real message and expected to do something different?

I arrived at the enemy camp, and the soldiers came out to meet me but in an unexpected way. Their spirit had changed from aggressive, threatening and warlike, to child-like, open, excited and full of wonder as I handed them the armor. They paid no attention to me but rather buzzed about the treasure they now had, amazed by it all, as if it contained some special magic.

I pondered that dream for many years, and it turned out I WAS missing the real message at the time. I came to see that the enemy that needs the armor of Christ, the armor of light if you will, lives within each of us in our disordered appetites and desires and passions. They fight a fierce battle against an intellect and will that have been dimmed and weakened by original sin. The heart has been reinforced in its disorder by our personal sinfulness and dysfunctional relationships. (Yet for me it was the heart that also responded first to grace.)

At the time, I was not fully aware of the habits of sin that were integrated into my life. Those habits were the fruit of victories frequently won by my disordered interior without much resistance from anywhere within me. So when Jesus told me to take His armor to the enemy, I began to see He was not referring to an outside force so much (though powers and principalities do fight against us) as the inside battle between good and evil, self-indulgence and self-sacrifice, generosity and selfishness, courage and cowardice, fear and trust, that waxes and wanes in the heart of every person with greater or lesser intensity.

Today, many people talk about beauty, truth, and goodness as routes of access to God since God Himself is perfect beauty, etc., and the source of these realities in which He manifests Himself. I believe though that there is something more fundamental that precedes the recognition of God through truth and beauty and goodness. That something is light, specifically the Christ Light.

"Now the earth was a formless void, there was darkness over the deep, with a divine wind sweeping over the waters. God said, 'Let there be light,' and there was light." Gen 1:2-3

This light is more primordial in a sense than the visible expression of beauty or truth or goodness which manifest a little later in creation. The light comes first. It is a fact we are always surrounded by beauty, truth and goodness, but I never saw it until God spoke those words into my own life: "Let there be light," and the light started to seep in.

Beauty, truth, and goodness emit their own light to be sure. But so few of us recognize real beauty, goodness or truth because we are not prepared to see it. We get stuck in the dark. Yet, the light of Christ searches us out and finds a way to break through. It begins changing things. It is this light that was present as creation came into being and it is the light that precedes our own re-creation in Christ.

My encounter with this light came directly from the face of Christ after a time of deep suffering. It was a light, a gaze that startled and then transfixed me in the middle of a life going nowhere. I recognized it as precious and to be protected and so did not speak about it to anyone for many years. It was also a light I began straining toward with all my might, like the germinated seed that finally breaks through the dirt that covers it and struggles for all its worth to rise.

I began reading the Word of God, the lamp unto my feet, every day, sitting quietly in the presence of Jesus in the Blessed Sacrament, attending daily Mass, slowly returning to the sacraments and devouring works like the *Confessions* of St. Augustine and Thomas Merton's *Seven Story Mountain*, which providentially landed in my path.

I didn't know much, but the Light of Christ, which bathed me during wordless adoration woke me up, caused things to begin growing in me that I did not know were there. I had a destiny to bear fruit I never knew was seeded in me in the first place.

This Light acts in much the same way, figuratively speaking, that photosynthesis in plants does. Green plants use sunlight to synthesize foods from the elements around them, carbon dioxide, and water. They then create life-giving oxygen as a by-product. The Light of Christ hits us in a similar way. Beauty, truth and goodness suddenly become visible, accessible, and able to feed us, enlighten us, cause and sustain growth and fruitfulness in us, helping us to come to a beautiful and healthy maturity.

Light often needs an opening to get in. This is a hidden beauty of suffering. It breaks us open, cracks us apart, exposes things we have buried which need the life-giving and healing power of the light.

If we allow ourselves more and more to be immersed in God's Light, our lives in Christ begin to generate essential elements, fresh air for others in the midst of spiritual famine and darkness. The light of God is everywhere and the children of light see it plainly (Wisdom 18)

Gathering the Light is a collection of articles, reflections and poetry. Many of the articles have appeared in various Catholic publications. It is set up in such a way that it can be used for personal reflection, book studies and support groups. We have been using a reflection from this collection every time we meet as the Facing Our Immortality cancer support group. In the midst of serious illness, or perhaps because of it, the desire to know the deep things of God becomes even more active and especially efficacious.

The format of *Gathering the Light* offers focal points of light meant to help us see what perhaps we have not seen before. Each article, with a few exceptions, hovers around one-thousand words. It is very manageable for the busy person trying to go a little deeper in his or her relationship with God. At the end, some questions for reflection are provided if needed.

Jesus tells us to put on His armor of light as we go out into the darkness of the times. But He also tells us that darkness is found in our own hearts, that out of our hearts come "evil thoughts— murder, adultery, sexual immorality, theft, false testimony, slander. 20 These are what defile a person." MT 15:19

It is the Christ light that penetrates through hard exteriors, through sin, through the grossness of our hearts, and draws the hiding soul out so it can shake off the shackles of darkness, and be transformed. Our lives are all to be like tracers in a night sky, lighting up both the battlefield we are on and the destination, the victory we seek to claim. Place yourself in the Light of Christ, in the glory that shines forth from His face and touches and changes every living thing on earth that receives it. Where the light is blocked, or we turn away, we will fail to thrive. Find the Light, gather the Light, stay in the Light, be a light for others... "The world and the Church need you to be beacons of light for the journey of the men and women of our time. This should be your prophetic witness. You have chosen not to flee the world out of fear, as some might think, but to remain in the world, while not being of the world-- Apostolic Constitution, *Vultum Dei quaerere*, "Seeking the face of God," July 22, 2016

Our God is a God of hope and promise.

"In the tender compassion of our God, the dawn from on high shall break upon us, to shine on those who dwell in darkness and the shadow of death and to guide our feet into the way of peace."

May it be so in each of our lives, and may we be the beacons of light, the tracers in the night sky for the redemption of our age.

Sr. Anne Marie, SOLT

Let there be light.

A LIFE FREELY LIVED

From the perspective of eternity, there is really only **one urgency: the salvation of souls.** Birthing souls into eternal life is a labor that is perhaps the most hidden, yet, most valuable labor of all. This is not the kind of work many people ever think of or even consciously involve themselves in. Yet when the weight of what is at stake is felt, and an eternity of either endless happiness or endless torment is understood within the depths of a soul, great hearts are moved in the likeness of Jesus' own heart to do whatever they can to keep even one soul from being lost.

A century ago, a group of men called the One-Way Missionaries, freely chose to serve that urgency by purchasing one-way tickets to remote parts of the earth where the Gospel had not yet been proclaimed, or where the Good News was treated with life-threatening hostility.

Those who volunteered to go did not expect to return, and most of them didn't. They packed their belongings into a coffin meant for their burial and set off to strange lands, willing to pay the highest price so that their forgotten brothers and sisters might know the surpassing greatness of Him Who calls us out of the darkness and into His marvelous light. (1 Peter 2:9)

One of the most famous One-Way Missionaries was a Scotsman named A. W. Milne, who volunteered to go to the New Hebrides in the South Pacific to live among tribal headhunters. He knew when he left that these tribes had already killed every missionary sent before him. And yet, something must have stirred Milne's heart with graces of Divine appointment and courage. He must have been able to utter the words of St. Paul about himself:

17

"I no longer live, but Christ within me lives." When that happens, the fire of Christ's passion for souls takes over and drives a person to go where they would never go otherwise.

Milne was the right missionary for the right time and place. He  lived among the tribal peoples for 35 years, and when he died, the people buried him in the center of the village and marked his grave with the following epitaph: **"When He Came There Was No Light. When He Left There Was No Darkness."**

What sentence would capture the story of our lives and reveal the level of our involvement with things that really matter? Can we win souls for Christ if every difficulty, every setback, every fierce battle causes us to whimper, to complain, to become discouraged, to crumble? Doesn't the enemy like to see soldiers who run, who hide, who desert because they don't believe the battle is worth the blessings it will obtain?

If the highest currency in the economy of Redemption is love freely willing to lay down its life for a brother or sister in danger of being lost eternally, how rich are we really? And how free are we really if we can't make the sign of the Cross in public or pray at a restaurant before eating because of what other people might think? Self-interest doesn't get us far in eternity. "Whoever seeks to preserve his life will lose it, but whoever loses it will save it." (Lk 17:33) Wrong choices lead to unhappy endings not just for ourselves but also for those that follow us.

On the bright side, it is possible to bring many souls to eternal happiness simply by loving them as best you can. A smile that pierces through the oppressive fog of loneliness, a friendly inquiry, a genuine assist in difficulty, a non-judging, concerned presence; these can be life-changing moments for people because they break through the dismal experiences life has taught them to expect, and stir hope, giving signs that life has better possibilities. Loving like this is not always easy. It can involve real sacrifice. But sacrifice is love in action and proof of its authenticity.

The real mission of Christ, of the Church, of ourselves, is not necessarily somewhere far away in a foreign land. Some will be called to foreign lands. But even for them, the real mission, as Pope Francis says, is the human person. "Today...every dimension of the human being is mission territory, awaiting the announcement of the Gospel." Christ's mission is all around us.

A soul that becomes able to completely lay down its life for others, in whatever form that takes, walks straight into heaven at the end of this life. Nothing holds it back or weighs it down. It goes immediately to its source in the Heart of God because it has already tasted and drunk freely of this life-giving love in its own life. This love is what changes the world and secures beatitude for all those who come in contact with it and receive it into themselves.

The Church and her mission of salvation will never lose relevance and will never be conquered. We either fight with her and for her through every storm no matter how severe or frightening, or we abandon her and ensure our own demise. Jesus doesn't ask us to spread the kingdom and fight for our brothers and sisters only if things are easy and perfect. He asks us to fight and stay faithful precisely because they aren't. He will do the rest.

Questions for Reflection

1. What determines my life? Success? Other people's opinions? God's Law? Self- Image?

2. Can I still be genuinely free even in the midst of illness or suffering?

3. How do I lay down my life for others? Where am I not really free in my life?

4. How have I experienced God's call to mission in my life?

Saints Damian and Marianne of Molokai,
in the midst of illness and suffering,
intercede for us.

DISCERNMENT IN THE MODERN AGE

One of the banes of modern life is the ubiquitous presence of bad entertainment, bad both in the sense of poorly crafted and in the sense of poisonous content. It's an observation that can be applied to books, movies, music, TV, and other forms of leisure activity as well. What constitutes healthy food for the mind and soul? We have great concern for the health of our bodies and our environment. And we feed them and protect them accordingly. At the same time, we seem to have much less conscious concern for what goes into our minds, our souls, our spirits. We simply consume whatever is offered, no longer recognizing the difference between junk food and delicacy, nutrients, and toxins.

This can be very dangerous. It's a lot like seeing a glass of cold, refreshing water after coming in on a hot, dusty day. The reaction is immediate and almost overwhelming. We would, without thinking, take the water and drink it. But if someone told us that despite its inviting appearance, the water had e-coli in it, we would not approach it, much less drink it, no matter how thirsty we were, knowing it would be hazardous to our health.

This is very much like what happens when we indiscriminately read or watch whatever is the latest rage, whether it be fictional stories, movies, TV shows that mock God, believers, our faith, or current book marketings of pornography (now especially targeting women's readership). So many times, people say: "it's not so bad. It's just a little sex, or just a little violence, or just a little language."

The reality, though, is that it doesn't matter whether the poison is hidden in small amounts. A little poison will kill you just as dead over time. When our emotions, our passions, our senses, apart from our intellect, make our decisions for us, we are capable of drinking to the dregs whatever contaminant is presented to us. And today, very deadly poisons abound. Our culture prizes acceptance, tolerance, and open-mindedness. It has been noted though, that the danger comes when people become so open-minded their brains fall out. Pope Benedict mentioned that knowledge for its own sake only leads to sadness, and sometimes, to much worse things.

This is not a new problem. The young St. Teresa of Avila had an attraction to the romance/adventure novels of her time, until she realized that the illusions, vanity and worldliness they sowed in her were a great obstacle to her life in general and her relationship with God in particular. They did not help her live in reality and especially in the reality of her dignity as a woman, a beloved daughter of God with a great destiny, a great part to play in the life of the Church and the world.

St. Ignatius of Loyola, Founder of the Jesuits, also had this problem before his conversion. He is famous for realizing how the books he read affected the movements of his soul, for better or worse. While recovering from a severe battle injury, he began to recognize that the worldly books he was fond of and which also fed his vanity gave him a feeling of excitement, which quickly passed and left him feeling discontented and restless. On the other hand, when he read books on the lives of the saints and their great deeds, he found himself inspired and filled with a desire to follow their example. These feelings did not change. From this simple observation St. Ignatius developed his principles for discernment, which are now indispensable teachings for anyone serious about the spiritual life.

We, of course, need discernment in many areas of our lives. And because we live in a complicated age, it is good to look for some general direction. One place to find this is back at the very beginning. God gave some straightforward instructions for life in the Garden, and repeated them after the fall, through Moses. He told Adam and Eve that they could eat from the Tree of Life and the other trees in the Garden, but not of the Tree of the Knowledge of Good and Evil. Later, He reiterated this directive to the Israelites in Exodus. "Choose life that you may live."

In all honesty, when our question becomes: "Is what I am about to say or see or do, life-giving to me and those around me," we can frame issues in a new light. This is not the only question we sometimes need to ask. But it is a very good place to start and finish. Is this life-giving or is this poison to me, to my relationships, to my dignity or someone else's dignity? It is a question that can be used with many of the choices we should make today with more deliberation than we do. And it is a question that avoids the dissembling of moral relativism. Something is either life-giving to all involved, or it is not. If it is not, it is to be avoided.

God's commandments and the Church's counsels are not meant to cramp our style or dampen our fun. They are meant to protect us. God knows what is good, what is healthy for us. And He also knows what will make us sick in body, mind, and spirit. Technology and the creative powers of mankind in many different fields have the potential to serve life or to bring death, both physical and spiritual death, depending on how they are used. If we genuinely want to live and live well the abundant life Jesus promises us, then we have to stop starving our own souls and start discerning how to eat more plentifully from the Tree of Life.

Questions for Reflection

1. Where in my life am I eating from the Tree of the Knowledge of Good and Evil instead of the Tree of Life?

2. What kinds of things does a person dealing with serious illness need to discern? Physically, spiritually, emotionally, psychologically?

3. What feeds me emotionally and spiritually when I am suffering or deeply challenged by life?

4. Have I ever sensed the mission and purpose of my life? If so, how have the challenges of life impacted that?

Saints Teresa of Avila and Ignatius of Loyola,
help us discern what is best for our souls.

STIRRING UP THE WATERS OF GRACE

ne of the most intriguing stories in the Gospel is the story of the crippled man waiting for healing at the Pool of Bethesda. The man has been suffering for 38 years but is unable to get to the pool fast enough when the angel comes to stir the waters. Jesus sees him and asks if he wants to be well. When the man expresses his desire for healing but his inability to reach it on his own, Jesus heals him on the spot. But then, Jesus later seeks out the now healed man to warn him about sin. He says: "Look, you are well; do not sin anymore, so that nothing worse may happen to you." Jn 1:14

This Lent, Jesus asks us the same question: 'Do you want to be well? Do you want to know where sin has crippled you, paralyzed you? And do you want to know true freedom?' Because Jesus comes to destroy the sickness of sin and the deformity it causes in our lives. We only have to desire it and choose it.

Many years ago, a friend shared a dream that deeply disturbed him. He was walking through a lovely forest when he came upon a clearing with a house in the middle of it. The house exerted a powerful pull on him. Everything within him wanted to go into that house. So he approached the screened-in porch, entered, and headed for the front door. As he walked up to the front door, someone came up to him and said: "Before you can go in, you have to eat this." He looked down to see a plate of dog excrement being handed to him.

He, of course, was upset that he could have had such a dream, not knowing at first what it could mean. But then, in a flash of insight, it became clear. The dream was an attempt to re-frame a profound struggle that had to do with an almost overpowering temptation to grave sin. Everything within him wanted to give in to the attraction of this particular sin. Yet his faith told him that if he gave in to this sin he would so defile himself that it would be like eating a plate of manure.

Sin is really that ugly. And it's an ugliness we give ourselves. The saints, on the other hand, tell us that a soul in the state of grace is beautiful beyond compare. That is the real beauty we should be seeking.

We often recognize that something is wrong within us, in the deep recesses of our being. We are attracted to things that are not good, things that enslave us, make us feel ugly about ourselves, and keep us from true freedom. And once we are bound, immobilized as it were, it takes an intervention of God's grace to free us. We cannot free ourselves.

Jesus comes to save us from sin and the effects of sin in our lives. We are not alone in this. The Gospel story says that there was a large number of ill, blind, lame, and crippled at the pool waiting for healing.

So how can we access the same healing Jesus so freely gives in the Gospels? Many ways are possible. But we are given three special gifts during Lent, which stir up the waters of grace in our lives. Prayer, Fasting, and Almsgiving. Prayer stirs up the grace we need for deeper healing in our rela-

tionship with God. Fasting brings the waters of grace down upon the disorder we have within ourselves. And Almsgiving opens up rivers of grace in our relationship to others.

Additionally, if you want to have the same direct encounter with Jesus that the crippled man had, start frequenting the sacrament of Penance and Reconciliation, and Holy Communion after that. Every sacrament contains within it a personal encounter with the living God Himself. Hence, every sacrament contains rivers of grace that can change us to the degree we let those waters flow.

Our deepest healing will always come first and foremost from eliminating sin in our lives. Sin always brings suffering, both personal and at the same time, upon the whole Body of Christ. There is no such thing as a private sin. As Our Lady of Fatima warned us over a century ago: war, something we often live in fear of, is a consequence of sin, both private sin and institutionalized, communal sin.

Every day we engage the battle against sin, against judgment, unforgiveness, promiscuity, pornography, dishonesty, infidelity, blasphemy, greed, self-righteousness, gossip, slander, unworthy Communions, anti-life acts, apathy, and every other attachment we have to our pet sins. Jesus spent 40 days in the desert fasting and conquering every temptation you or I would ever have so we could conquer those same temptations in our own lives. The choice is beauty over ugliness, freedom over enslavement, self-denial over sin, happiness over temporary pleasure, shame, and guilt. We, too, have to answer the question of Jesus: "Do you really want to be well?"

Questions for Reflection

1. Jesus tells us that not all sickness is a result of personal sin. Yet it is an undeniable truth that sin causes suffering, both personal and communal. What are your observations of this in the world? In your own life?

2. Do you think there are actually people who don't want to be well? Why would that be?

3. How does Jesus heal? And for what ultimate purpose?

4. Why does Jesus leave some people with their suffering?

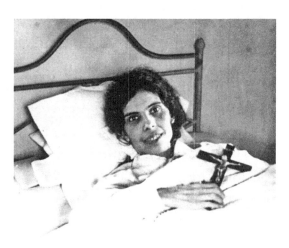

Blessed Alexandrina of Balazar,
teach us to unite our sufferings with Jesus on the cross.

OUR LADY OF CONQUERING LOVE

At Calvary, where Jesus conquered sin, the flesh, the devil, death, and all of hell,** Mary was given to us to be our Mother. In His last moments, Jesus shared His love for Mary with us that we might love her too and entrust ourselves to her care just as He did. It is a love upon which He bestows boundless blessing.

Mary is not a passive woman, nor a pushy, aggressive one either. This is the valiant woman par excellence, who is as active a mother in the world today as she was when she mothered all those Jesus gave to her care during His hidden life, His public ministry, and in the early Church as it struggled through persecution to establish itself and evangelize the world.

One of the great stories of Our Lady's care for us, from our recent history, comes to us from the Philippines. The Philippines is a poor country, and the trials and sufferings of its people are immense. At the same time the people have a vibrant, living faith that freely expresses itself in their culture.

During the 1980s, after having suffered for 20 years under

the corrupt, oppressive, authoritarian regime of President Ferdinand Marcos, the Archbishop of Manila and spiritual leader of Asia, Jaime Cardinal Sin, called for a Marian year. People attended Rosary rallies, processions and special Masses by the millions, imploring Our Blessed Mother's help.

At end of the year (1986), the people, including Priests and Religious, took to the streets, again by the millions, praying, carrying banners, and demanding that Marcos step down. Marcos responded by sending tanks into the streets and ordering his soldiers to fire upon the crowds. The soldiers looked into their gun sights to take aim but saw images of Our Lady everywhere. They could not, would not fire. In the end, Marcos was airlifted out of the country, and democracy was restored.

This was an unheard-of thing, a completely bloodless, non-violent revolution. Secular media called it the People Power Revolution. The Spanish of another era, here in our own country, would have called it the work of *La Conquistadora*, Our Lady of Conquering Love! And the Filipinos themselves know where the real victory came from.

St. Pope John Paul II took his cue from the events in the Philippines and called for a Marian year for the whole world from June 7 (Pentecost), 1987 to August 15 (the Assumption), 1988. Following the close of the world-wide Marian year, the Iron Curtain fell, and shortly thereafter, the Soviet bloc disintegrated, all to the utter astonishment of the secular press.

Coincidence? Don't believe it! They say the most common word heard on the battlefield is "mother." But this is the Mother we need in the battles we fight today. We are all her children, and she is ready to help any who approach her.

Praying the rosary, asking Mary's intercession, and honoring her in different ways has so much more efficacy and meaning when we know and understand her as she really is. Mary is more favored, has a richer personality, more gifts, deeper emotions, higher wisdom, more profound graces, more sensitive, loving virtue, and a more heavenly human beauty than anyone who ever was or ever will be born, aside from Jesus himself. No one sways the heart of God nor reaches it as quickly as she does. And no one apart from God Himself loves us as much as she does!

She is ours! This is who God has given us to be our Mother, the very one He singled out and prepared for Himself. This is the woman of unshakable faith in the midst of suffering and sorrows we will never even remotely comprehend or appreciate. This is a woman of invincible charity, hope, and courage, who comes up from the desert, like an army in battle array, and crushes the head of the ancient enemy with her heel. Her humility, simplicity, and modesty are more feared by the powers of darkness than the greatest preaching on earth! This is the soul so full of grace and light and adorned with such great fruits that it alone ravishes the heart of God and causes Him to send floods of grace upon the whole world, beginning with the greatest gift of all, the sending of Jesus to be our Savior.

With grateful hearts, we ask Mary Our Mother, Our Lady of Conquering Love, to obtain for each of us the Light, charity, and strength that routs the enemy, overcomes the immense dangers of our present existence, and helps us in peace to continue the work of building the Kingdom of God.

Questions for Reflection

1. What exactly is love meant to conquer?

2. How do you see God's love at work in your life?

3. Is suffering compatible with love?

4. If perfect love casts out all fear (1 Jn 4:18) where, in my life, does love need to grow?

Our Lady of Conquering Love,
banish the darkness; vanquish the foe.

GOD'S DREAM AND THE FULLNESS OF TIME

In the beginning, before light split the darkness for the first time and the waters were gathered into life-giving bodies; before the winds were purposefully directed and the stars and planets assigned their places, before any vegetation or land formation or animals were considered in the mind of God, we were His dream. The Father's vision of a shared life with us, shattered in the Garden, awaited a new fullness of time. When the acceptable time came, "when peaceful stillness encompassed everything and the night in its swift course was half spent, God's all-powerful Word leapt from heaven's royal throne into the doomed land" and the darkness of our hearts Wisdom 18:15-17.

At the first Christmas, the whole world is in movement. Mary and Joseph travel to Bethlehem to be counted in the census. They journey, at the same time, toward the moment in which God, in the Person of Jesus, will enter the world through the womb of Mary, to live out His dream of a shared life of communion and intimacy with us.

The Father knows the price He will pay for His dream. Mary, in Her mother's heart and her knowledge of the Scriptures, knows it too. Her Son, Who shall be called the Messiah, the Christ, the Son of the Most High, will also be known as the Suffering Servant who will give his life up as a ransom for the many.

God enters our world in the fullness of time because He can

 no longer wait to be with us in Person. But Christmas also comes because mankind, in the persons of Mary and Joseph, the shepherds and the wise men, seek God as well; because the intense, hidden longing of their souls has not been misinterpreted to them by the false prophets of the world. Their interior has not been cluttered with distraction. It is unfettered by illusion. God is their inner life and moves them in a mutual, eager longing, in silence, in poverty, in simplicity, in penetrating light and redeeming love so that His dream and our everlasting happiness can be realized.

In every age, in the life of every person, this same movement is recapitulated. Christmas reminds us of this in a singular way. For we too are moving on a journey through this life, in company with millions of others, to our own definitive encounter with God, a God Who has beckoned us to the deepest friendship and Who offers the gift of eternal joy to us by coming into the night of our world, our hearts, our souls, in the trappings of our own poverty, helplessness and littleness.

Mary and Joseph "walk the way of perfection" to Bethlehem because they know God, and they understand, in the hidden depths of their hearts, the dream He has for all mankind. They call us to follow this way with them. It is a path that holds difficulty, discomfort, the contempt of the world, but which brings us also to be the friends of God, as the psalmist says: "He who walks the way of perfection shall be my friend." Ps 101

On Christmas night, Angel voices will beckon us to follow

them to the stable where Eternal Love pierces through the veil of separation to reclaim His children, those starved for light and battered by the darkness of sin. As a tiny babe, He comes. He comes to feed the hollow faces of the hopeless with joy and surface the hidden grief that devours in silence, in order to heal in love.

In Bethlehem, two longings meet and answer each other: the longing of God and the yearning of man. May this Christmas find us fulfilling the dream of God's own heart in the lowly stable of our own souls. May He find in us the warmth and love and union that has been His dream from before time began.

Questions for Reflection

1. What is the dream you have for your life?

2. Have you ever considered what God's dream for your life might be? Don't be generic in your answer. God loves you personally, and His plans for you are unique.

3. Are you aware of the deepest yearning of your own heart? What is it centered in? Yourself, the world, others, or God?

4. How would you describe your experience of Advent and Christmas over the years? Deeper every year or distracted, superficial, and ruled by the commercialism of the season in the secular order?

Mary and Joseph, lead us in walking
the way of perfection.

MARY, MOTHERHOOD AND THE FAMILY OF GOD

Mary's motherhood, like motherhood in general, was **lived out quietly behind the scenes.** St. Pope John Paul II pointed out that "History is written almost exclusively as the narrative of men's achievements, when in fact its better part is most often molded by women's determined and persevering action for good." (*Papal Message On Women's Conference to Mrs. Gertrude Mongella.* May 1995)

Mary achieved more than any other human being. This was done in the most intimate way in the context of Her Divine Motherhood, a role which God asked her to live, and which She joyfully assented to! She continues to bring souls to life in grace and to love saints into being, so essential and eternal is Her motherhood to who She is.

But just as God took His flesh from the body of Mary, so every child comes into this world through the body of a mother. Every conception is a kind of annunciation, God asking permission of the woman to bring a new life into the world because His creative love has delighted in the thought of that particular and unique little one. He "entrusts the human person to her in a special way" (JPII) and asks every woman's immediate care and participation in the formation of the life He gives. Just as He sent His own Son to be His ultimate gift to a world dying from sin, so He sends every child to be a gift to a world in desperate need of His goodness.

Some are meant to show the face of Christ's mercy, others His compassion. Some will be teachers in His likeness; others will bring his miracles into people's lives. Others will spend and consume themselves to heal and unite us all into one Family of Our Father.

Every mother wants greatness for her child. That greatness will be measured by the part they play in the greatest drama ever, the drama of redemption, the battle for souls, the struggle for the brothers and sisters of the age we live in. The call on every life is to participate in redeeming its own age. Every gift of Christ made Incarnate in the lives of those born into this world is meant to serve this.

It should be no surprise then that the attack on family is so strong today. We have an enemy who fights ferociously to keep us from living the image and likeness of God, especially as mothers and fathers. He hates the reflection of the Incarnation in every newborn child. And he despises the communion of Trinitarian love that each family is called to live.

Mothers have a particular answer to this which is seen most clearly in the life of our Blessed Mother at the foot of the Cross. In Christ, all the joys and sufferings, sorrows, and glories of motherhood are taken up into His own Mystery and become redemptive. Archbishop Fulton Sheen puts it this way:

> The pains which a woman bears in labor help to expiate the sins of mankind, and draw their meaning from the Agony of Christ on the Cross. Mothers are, therefore, not only co-creators with God; they are co-redeemers with Christ in the flesh. (*Three to Get Married*)

There is likewise a Eucharistic reflection which St. John Chrysostom notes: "As a woman nourishes her child with her own blood and milk, so does Christ unceasingly nourish with his own blood those to whom He himself has given life."

If we are to imitate Christ and become one with him in all things, Motherhood is truly a privileged place where, with Christ, a woman can say: "This is my body which is given up for you." The tragedy today is that so many women are saying instead: "This is my body, and I will not give it up for you." They have not seen nor understood the greatness of their calling.

The work of pointing the way and leading people to the kingdom that is not of this world is not easy. It requires death to self. But God takes even the most insignificant daily realities and makes them fruitful in this work. Mary did for Jesus every day what all mothers do for their children, dressing them, washing them, feeding them, teaching them. It is hidden work but has immeasurable value.

Mothers know this better than others. They not only live out the Paschal Mystery in their own flesh and spirit, but they also live it out for and with their children. Their boundless love bleeds redeeming grace into the lives of their sons and daughters. Mary is the most profound example of this. But it is clearly seen in the lives of women like St. Monica, St. Gianna Molla, St. Elizabeth Ann Seton, and countless mothers whose lives will never be known to anyone outside of their immediate circles, until they get to heaven that is, where they will be honored and esteemed for their deep and faithful participation in the creation of God's own Family.

Human motherhood, along with human fatherhood, comes directly from the hand of God. Both are, in fact, a reflection of and participation in God's Fatherhood, which is Divine. When God created man He considered what would be the human expression

of the life He Himself lives. His answer was Family and family constituted as mother, father, and children.

In the simplicity of God, our life on earth is meant to be about what our life in heaven will be like. The real stars in heaven will be mothers, for without their "yes" to our existence, none of us would have a chance of going there. But the supreme star will be our Queen, our Mother Mary whose "yes" to God's love gave us our Savior and Redeemer, the chance to call God our Father, and the gift that every heart longs for: to live in the perfect family forever.

Questions for Reflection

1. What was your experience with your own mother and how were you affected by it? What word would you use to describe her character?

2. What has happened to motherhood today?

3. Why is motherhood and the maternal spirit so crucial to civilization?

4. What are some of the hidden achievements of women, mothers?

"O Jesus, I promise to submit myself
to all that You permit to happen to me;
only make me know your will."
St. Gianna Molla

40

CATHOLIC EDUCATION AND THE ONE THING NECESSARY

The greatest moment of our lives, and usually the one we are least prepared for, is the one in which, upon leaving this world and entering the next, we will find ourselves face-to-face with God. In a real sense, we will judge ourselves in the presence of His pure goodness, love, beauty, light, and truth. And we will immediately know where we belong.

Our judgment will occur in the context of two realities Jesus points to in the Gospel: how we have loved (I was hungry…) and how we have used the gifts God has given us. (Have we buried or hidden them under a bushel basket or used them to help build the Kingdom?) In the end, at this definitive moment, that's what will matter.

So how can we prepare so that this moment will be for us one of utter joy and anticipation? Enter the deepest purpose of Catholic education, which begins first and foremost in the home with the parents as the primary educators of their children. The ultimate goal of all Catholic education, whether in the home, school, Church, or out in the world, is to prepare us to, one day, see God face-to-face, having helped us to recognize and fulfill our own personal destiny in God's great plan for mankind!

Even the most mundane subjects are meant, ultimately, to serve this goal, for everything that exists and that we interact with here has its connection to God, and either reveals something about Him directly or something about what He has created and why. In my early teaching years, the children, because they were in an environment which encouraged it, continually and spontaneously made these connections in music class, math class, science studies, geography, etc. It didn't matter. They quite easily saw: "Middle C is just like Jesus. He's the center to everything!" Or, "no matter what you are doing, God the Father looks into your heart to see if His Son is there!"

The development of Catholic education, which in a real sense, began in the monasteries, gives us a fundamental key to understanding the direction Catholic education should have today. For the monks, the essentials were always the same: "the supreme good of knowing Christ Jesus" (Phil 3:8), in light of which all else is rubbish.

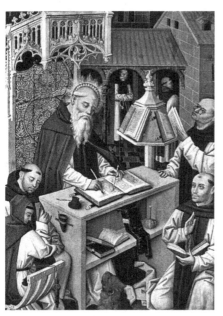 The establishment of monastic communities was therefore ordered to a life that was conducive to the finding of God and to living out a covenantal relationship with Him. The biblical principles by which the monks lived and their deep study and contemplation of the mysteries of God in creation, started to leaven the chaos around them, so that time, learning, art, science, music, animal husbandry, farming, care of the poor, all began to be marked by the laws and light which God Himself had put into creation. An order and a fruitfulness developed that had heavenly origins. The bells announcing the call to prayer, which punctuated each day, and the liturgical seasons with their abundance of solemnities, feasts, and even the rich Gospel lessons of ordinary time, made the meaning of life, one's responsibilities, one's destiny, readily understood. It is important to note that Monasticism did not begin as an at-

tempt to create a new culture or civilization. The holy men and women of early times were interested in the one thing necessary. The impact upon the surrounding environs was entirely in accord with the words of Christ: "Seek first the kingdom (of God) and his righteousness, and all these things will be given you besides." (Mt 6:33)

Catholic education should be a response to the loss of this vision. C. Houselander noted in her book, *Guilt* that "the great repression of our age is the repression of Christ in man." (ch.8). Nowhere is this more evident than in secular education. We live in a time that has known Christ and now rejects him. We cannot wonder that man no longer understands himself. Apart from Christ, it is not possible.

The Christ-life within is still the essential thing amid the contemporary bombardment of the inessential and our own growing barbarism. With authentic education, children begin to become (not in a forced way, but a supernaturally natural development), little Christs touching the world in the activities of their childhood and adolescence. In adulthood, as they grow into the full measure of the mature Christ, they are meant to move into all the realms of human activity: intellectual, physical, scientific, academic, artistic, apostolic, spiritual, etc. and to be, even greater leaven as they take their places in the world.

Pope St. John Paul II often pointed out that the Church and the world are at a crossroads. Catholic education must respond to this challenge with new vigor. When it stays true to itself, it is the key to the formation of the new man, a new humanity and a new Pentecost, for, we know, "a Christian has only to be, in order to change the world." C. Dawson, *Christianity and the New Age.*

Questions for Reflection

1. How did you experience the purpose of education in your own life?

2. What do you observe of education in the current culture?

3. What is the link between authentic education and Christ?

4. How can education be brought to serve the development of the whole person, body, soul, and spirit?

Saint John Bosco, teach us to teach.

THE PRICE
OF OUR RANSOM

What does God think of humanity? What does God think of us? There is plenty of evidence to suggest that what we think He thinks and what He actually thinks are often two very different things.

The bloodshed in the last century alone causes devout people sometimes to feel God should intervene, and perhaps, just as in the time of Noah, start over with a remnant. After all, wars and ideological struggles, the persecution of Christians in various parts of the world, genocide, tyranny and intentional famines, homicide, and the holocaust that is abortion have been responsible for the deaths of 1.5 - 2 billion people in only one century. There is not a place on earth that has been unaffected by senseless bloodshed, a situation which at times seems almost hopeless, even to people of strong faith.

Yet, If one could look from some distant point in the universe, at all the suns birthing worlds, all the planets spinning through space, at nebulae and quasars, pulsars, comets, moons and asteroids, the prodigious wonders of galaxies coming to life and others passing away, there would be one spot in creation more beautiful, more blessed, more full of light than all the rest! And it would be our own earth.

This is not because of those who inhabit this world. The inhabitants of our particular world are often so caught in quagmires of darkness that they cannot be said to be responsible in any way for this beauty. Yet exceptional beauty there is because of God's presence among us.

God's interventions in human history are respectful, astounding, and full of wisdom we do not readily comprehend. Most of the things we attribute to God, war chief among them, are the consequences of our own sins catching up with us. But from the beginning of time, God's response to our sin, after pointing out the consequences which logically flowed from them, was to promise a Redeemer. The first sin led all of us into captivity. But God was immediately prepared to pay the ransom.

Historically the amount of ransom demanded is determined by the value placed on the person held. The largest ransom ever paid was by the Incas in 1532, to Francisco Pizarro for the release of their leader. The amount of gold given him would be worth about $2 billion in today's markets. Pizarro took the ransom but did not honor the agreement. He executed the Incan leader anyway.

The ransom paid by God for us is infinitely beyond any sum. That in itself tells us something of the value God places on each one of us. St. Peter says:

> "You know that you were ransomed from the futile ways inherited from your fathers, not with perishable things such as silver or gold, but with the precious blood of Christ, like that of a lamb without blemish or spot." (1Peter 1:18-19).

Jesus gives His very life, down to His last drop of blood, to redeem us.

July is a month which the Church dedicates to honoring the Precious Blood of Jesus in a special way. Why the Precious Blood? Because the Precious Blood of Jesus is the price of our salvation. It is God's answer to our sin. It is the ransom He freely and willingly gives as an expression of His unfathomable love for us.

And this ransom, which is of infinite worth, has been paid once and for all. It may be claimed for anything and anyone, for salvation, conversions, protection, liberation from bondage, reconciliation, purification, healing, restoration of relationships with the Trinity, the saints, each other, for the souls in Purgatory, for advancement of the work of the Kingdom.

How do we access this ransom that is ours? Most easily through the sacraments, through the Mass, through prayer. St. Paul says that where sin abounds grace superabounds. (Romans 5:20). He can say this because of the ransom which Christ has paid! We are entitled to all the good things of God because of this ransom. And we are left all of the channels in the Church by which we may acquire them.

Who doesn't want to be saved? Saved from despair, saved from meaninglessness, rescued from a life without love, rescued from our own narrow, selfish desires and compulsions, and from all the captivities the world so easily lures us into? Is there anyone who does not want to be extricated from illusion and sin? Is there anyone who does not want to be saved from death? Really?

St. Pope John XXIII stated:

> The world can still set itself right and always will be able to, because the voice and Blood of Christ cry out for pity and mercy... Devotion to the Precious Blood is the devotion of our time...It is devotion for all souls, for the whole world.

If you really want to know what God thinks of humanity, what He thinks of you, ponder well the astounding price Christ has paid for you and for all of mankind, and let your heart respond unceasingly with awe and overflowing gratitude!

Questions for Reflection

1. How do you think God looks at humanity today?

2. How do we avoid projecting our own thoughts and judgments about others and about circumstances, onto God?

3. What is the power of the Blood of Christ all about? Why does Pope Saint John XXIII say it is the devotion meant for our time?

Pope Saint John XXIII,
impress upon us the power of the Blood of Christ.

PRINCIPALITIES AND POWERS

Our life in time is pretty simple. We live in the midst of a war that God in His mercy doesn't let us see completely. Were we to see some of what goes on in the invisible realms we would probably die of fright. Yet, the battle between good and evil is a part of our daily existence.

"For our struggle is not with flesh and blood but with the principalities, with the powers, with the world rulers of this present darkness, with the evil spirits in the heavens. Therefore, put on the armor of God, that you may be able to resist on the evil day, having done everything, to hold your ground." Eph 6: 12-13

In the wake of the current crisis in the Church, there are two questions each of us must ask.

1. How does God want me to respond to this?

2. How does the devil want me to respond to this?

We can quickly and correctly surmise that the devil wants us to become destructively enraged, fall into discouragement, rash judgment, accusation, despair, and justify ourselves into leaving the Church altogether. But, we can also look to Jesus to see how He responded.

Jesus chose 12 Apostles, men specially selected by Him for the specific work of establishing the Church, which He promised us would endure even though all hell come up against it. One of those men betrayed Jesus for a lousy sum of silver. Jesus called him friend even then, in one last effort to reclaim him.

Another, the future head of the infant Church, denied him three times. Jesus gave him the opportunity to recant by professing his love three times.

All the rest abandoned Him in his greatest need, out of fear. One only returned to the Cross because Our Lady gave him the courage to accompany her there. Jesus appeared to them all after rising from the dead, spoke peace to them, and after banishing their fear, prepared them to become mighty instruments in the hands of the Holy Spirit.

At the same time, Jesus does not go lightly on those who violate the innocence of children or remain obstinate in grave sin. "Better for them had they never been born." But it doesn't leave us off the hook either.

If only it were all so simple! If only there were evil people somewhere insidiously committing evil deeds, and it were necessary only to separate them from the rest of us and destroy them. But the line dividing good and evil cuts through the heart of every human being. And who is willing to destroy a piece of his own heart?" (Aleksandr I. Solzhenitsyn, *The Gulag Archipelago*)

The weapons of warfare against the evil in the heart of man have been laid out for us by Jesus in the Gospel: prayer, fasting (which the Fathers of the Church considered a form of exorcism), vigilance, self-denial and humility, humility, humility. Mary sends the devils fleeing in terror precisely for this reason. Her profound humility drew heaven to earth! It is the greatest power against the ugly pride that infects us all, a pride that is the gateway to so many other sins.

St. Ignatius picks up these themes in his classic meditation on The Two Standards. We are either in one camp or the other, the Lord's or Satan's. It is necessary for us to know what ground we stand on. Because in the end, holiness, communion with Christ, is the only thing that transforms the human heart and changes the world.

The devil told St. John Vianney, "If there were three such priests as you, my kingdom would be ruined. ..." That holiness, which should be the aspiration of every priest, is, at the same time, required of each of us as well. Our holiness as a people who come to live with and in and through Christ will then be the driving force behind the victories of the Kingdom of Light over the Kingdom of darkness in this present age. And that holiness will mark the glory of the world that is to come.

Questions for Reflection

1. Vatican II noted that modern man lives in a kind of duplicity, often identifying himself as Christian, but living as though he doesn't believe. Where do you find yourself? Which camp are you in? Or do you try to stay on the fence?

2. How does pride manifest itself in your life?

3. Do you recognize the particular strategies the devil uses on you? Are you aware of the weaknesses you have that make you vulnerable to his attacks?

4. Can you say holiness is the genuine aspiration of your life? What does holiness mean to you?

Saint John Vianney,
train us to wield the weapons of light
to conquer the forces of darkess.

WOMEN
AND THE
PRIESTHOOD

There is a question that still seems to be unsettled in the minds of many ordinary Catholics. It is a question that comes up when people positively assess our new Holy Father but think he still does not go far enough. The question: Why can't women be Priests?

Many of the responses given to this question seem, in the end, to fall back solely upon authority. Pope Paul VI said that respect for the modern mind requires more than this.

To shed light on the questions of the present, St. Pope John Paul II often led us back to the beginnings, to reflect on God's creation of man and woman before the fall. It is incontestable that both man and woman were created in the image and likeness of God. Both are equal in dignity because of this. But this does not make them the same in every other respect. They are two different expressions of the human person, created to live in unity with

one another, via a complementarity that assists them to reflect in some respect, the inner life of the Persons of the Trinity.

Further, Pope Saint John Paul the Great said, in one of his many engaging teachings on man and woman, that the closer a person comes to God, the more he or she become either mother or father. This is because God is Father. And both human motherhood and human fatherhood are reflections of God's Fatherhood which is divine.

So women are meant to be mothers and men fathers. But there is a deep understanding required here. All men and all women are meant to be mothers and fathers, regardless of whether they are married, single, religious or ordained.

This means that a woman is not a mother simply because she has born a child or has a body capable of bearing children. She is called to be a mother because in her spirit she is maternal, and the physical realities of her body simply correspond to the deeper spiritual principle of her being. Likewise, men are not called to be fathers simply because they have bodies capable of begetting children. They are called to be fathers because in their spirits they are paternal. Their bodies, too, simply manifest the deeper spiritual principles of their being.

Sts. Louis & Zelie Martin

We know that the Church is a family, God's family. Mothers and fathers are the essential elements for any family regardless of what the world says in its attempts to redefine family. Unless the paternal meets the maternal, life cannot be conceived, born, nor can it be nurtured to maturity. This is true in both the natural order and in the spiritual order, as well.

In the Church, this distinction is sometimes referred to as the Petrine and Marian dimensions. St. Peter, the Pope, Bishops, Priests are called to be spiritual fathers to the whole people of God, and therefore need to be men. But mothers are also essential to this order, and Mary, religious and all women, fill this role. In fact, the Church herself is called mother. It is why the Church has been stressing the importance of women so much, speaking about the feminine genius and the need for a greater presence of women and their gifts in the Church and in the world. It is the dimension that has not been understood or appreciated as well as it needs to be.

Paul Evdokimov, a famous Russian Orthodox theologian who was an official observer at Vatican II, said that without woman God cannot be born into the world. In the Incarnation, Jesus takes His flesh from the body of a woman. God establishes His link with humanity through maternity. This is a divine order that has not changed. Pope St. John Paul II pointed out that because of the mystery of the Incarnation, Jesus links Himself with every human being who comes into the world. And in the order intended by God, that is, through the body of a woman.

We know that the Priest brings Jesus to us in the Eucharist and in the sacraments. Yet if God calls us even before we are born (see Jeremiah) then there would be no Priests without women who give birth to them in the first place and nurture the life of God within them.

Ven. Margherita Occhiena
(Mother of St. John Bosco)

The life of grace received from Priests in the sacraments also often needs this maternal care. A close friend confessed that before her conversion she was caught in an adulterous relationship she could not break. She knew it was wrong and took it to Confession a number of times. But within a week she was always back in the relationship. She finally got a Priest in Confession who told her she needed to find someone to walk her through it, someone she could call and talk to every time she was tempted to go back. She befriended a religious woman, opened up to her, and after some time, was able to completely break things off. What was going on? She received grace in the sacrament, but it was like a seed that needed nurturing and strengthening in her soul. Once it was rooted and grew, through contact with her friend, she became strong enough to withstand the temptations. That is the maternal charism in action. Hidden perhaps, but essential to both our natural and spiritual lives.

On one occasion I was challenged by a group of seventh-grade girls on this issue of women in the priesthood. When the reality of the Church as the family of God was explained, and when the need for mothers and fathers was spoken about, there was no further argument. Too many of them came from single-parent families where they would've given anything to have had a mother and a father. They didn't want their mother to be their father or their father to be their mother even though a mother can do many things a father can, and vice versa. They wanted a family with both. And they knew experientially and sadly that without both, something fundamental in their lives was missing.

In a beautiful passage, Saint John Paul II says:

> Mary was not called to the ministerial priesthood, but the mission she received had no less value than a pastoral ministry. Indeed it was quite superior. She received a maternal mission at the highest level, to be the mother of Jesus Christ, and thus *Theotokos* the mother of God. This mission would broaden into motherhood for all men and women in the order of grace, and the same can be said of the mission of motherhood that women accept in the Church. They are placed by Christ in the wondrous light of Mary which shines at the summits of the Church and creation.

We must have ultimate respect for the dignity of the ministerial Priesthood. But if women truly understood the magnificence and greatness of their own calling and the urgent need which the world has for their gifts, they would not be interested in trading it for a false equality.

Questions for Reflection

1. It has been said that maternal love is the most powerful force on earth. Do you agree? Why or why not?

2. What do you think is the real issue behind the clamor for women priests?

3. Identify the gifts of woman that the world cannot live without.

4. What have you observed of the state of womanhood in the present culture?

Saint Catherine of Siena,
inspire all women to truly understand
their maternal charism
and the magnificence of their calling.

Behold Man Without God
William Kurelek

THE WINE
THAT DAZES

Recently, while speaking with a dear friend, I found **myself sharing** some of my personal experiences growing up during the 60's and 70's. I lived my grade school, high school, and college, during the great movements and turmoil of that time: the civil rights movement with its urban riots, massive and active anti-war, anti-establishment activity especially on the campuses, women's liberation, changes in the Church with Vatican II and shortly thereafter, the exodus of thousands of Priests and Sisters from their vocations. I vividly recall the assassinations of President John F. Kennedy, Martin Luther King Jr. and Robert F. Kennedy, from the impressionable and uncomprehending perspective of youth. My friend asked me what I thought, out of all that, had had the most significant impact on our culture, our society today. While there is a case to be made for the progress we've made in civil rights, and while I believe the Church has been tremendously blessed by Vatican II (yet is also still reeling from the effect of the thousands who left their vocations,) I responded that the sexual revolution, to my mind, has had the greatest impact on where we are today.

In the Divine Office, which Priests and Religious and many Laity pray daily, there is a psalm that speaks about what happens when God's people are unfaithful. Psalm 60: 5 says:

> You have inflicted hardships on your people and made us drink a wine that dazed us.

But then it says:

You have given those who fear you a sign to flee from the enemy's bow."

I was moved to ask what is the wine that dazes us? It seemed to me that the wine we tasted in the sexual revolution was the wine of sexual permissiveness. And now we crave this wine. We, as a people, have become addicted to this wine and over these last decades have brewed some very potent varieties of it. Some are so potent that they say one taste (pornography comes to mind), immediately hooks you.

In the space of a relatively short time, we have become like the chronic alcoholic who rationalizes his use and denies the devastation and destruction all around him, because he wants free and unfettered access. Never mind that marriages and families are destroyed, babies aborted, children traumatized and stripped of their innocence. Never mind that violence against women increases, along with every other imaginable form of degradation and perversion. Never mind that disease, physical, mental, emotional, and spiritual, can be directly traced to the devastating effects of this addiction. We just have to have it. We tell ourselves this makes us free, adult, normal, uninhibited. This is exactly what the alcoholic says.

Our denial with regard to what we are drinking is so strong now, that we are blind to our own enslavement, except when the despair this creates in us sometimes seeps through to the surface, and we experience that sin has its own punishment built right into it. We can no longer help ourselves. And because we do not want to be judged, we try to convince everyone else this is a good thing. "Try it; you'll like it." Thus have we exported the wine of our own lewdness to the nations, as the book of Revelation puts it. (Aren't we the biggest exporter of pornography in the world?)

This is one addiction that also paralyzes this country and

makes it passive, indifferent in the face of the grave moral challenges we face. We complicitly acquiesce to the sin of others so we can be left alone with our own sin.  "As long as you leave me free to do what I want, go ahead and do whatever you want." That seems to be the thinking of so many. It accounts for the apathy that exists in place of a vigorous defense of justice and right and all that is good, true and holy. How can there be moral indignation in people who are not living moral lives? Could this be why so many people are silent in the face of the gross attacks on human life and dignity that exist in our world today?

Psalm 60 says that God gives those who fear Him a sign to flee from the enemy's bow (the fiery darts St. Paul talks about). Perhaps one sign can be found in the Wedding Feast of Cana.

Jesus wants to give us a different kind of wine, the wine from this wedding feast. This wine is given to those who are rightly ordered in the gift of their sexuality and who celebrate it in the context in which it was given to us by Our Heavenly Father. This wine, the best wine, fills us with love for life, excitement at the promise it holds, joy in the divine love it expresses. It is a wine which is available to all, and which can be had by following Our Lady's counsel: "Do whatever He tells you."

This is the wine the world truly craves, the wine we were created to drink freely. This is the wine that will not enslave but will bring all of us into the true freedom of the sons and daughters of God. May the Most Holy Trinity and Our Lady heal us and bring us to be worthy to receive this wine.

Questions for Reflection

1. Pornography is very really the desecration of the image of God in another human being. And it is a degradation of that image in the person who participates in it. How can the sacredness of the image and likeness of God in another person be conveyed to children early on?

2. Though there are more serious sins than sins of the flesh (intellectual sins of pride for instance), yet, Our Lady at Fatima said more people go to hell because of sins of the flesh than any other kind of sin. How do we protect, immunize ourselves against this fiery dart? What can be done if you have been stung by this dart already?

3. How do we deal with the denial of harm that this activity causes? What is at the root of people's rejection of traditional morality today?

4. What do you observe of the presence of spiritual warfare in the world today? In the Church? In your own life?

5. The Gospel is full of stories and encounters where Jesus freed people from the oppression of the evil one, through healing, deliverance, etc. Has He done that in any way in your own life?

Saint John, put us on our guard against drinking the devil's toxic concoctions.

OF BILLBOARDS, PROPHECY, AND RESURRECTION

If you have traveled national highways much over the last decade, you may have noticed a battle of the billboards: Believers vs. atheists. Believers post things like: " The Fool Has Said in His Heart there is no God." "Life is Short. Eternity Isn't."–God "To All Our Atheist Friends: Thank God You're Wrong!"

Atheists post things like: "Don't believe in God? You are not alone." "In the Beginning Man Created God." And, "Want a Better World? Prayer Not Required."

These signs are obviously very public postings with specific intent. But there is room to wonder what these signs tell us about the age we live in. There is no doubt that western society has adopted a militant spirit against believers. But not all believers. God forgive us, but we are not bothered by believers in abortion, believers in freedom to pursue every type of perversity, believers in almost any kind of religion, even violent ones. We are not bothered by believers in systems or ideologies that consistently degrade or offend against human dignity. But we are "bothered" by believers in Jesus Christ! We are bothered by His effect on people, His power to persuade people, to influence them, to change their lives.

It points, in a timeless way, to the story of the Passion narrative, which we have just celebrated these last days. Caiaphas, the high priest involved in the orchestration of Jesus' execution, unwittingly prophesies the real significance of Jesus' death.

As the Sanhedrin met, the argument went like this: "What are we going to do? If we leave him (Jesus) alone, all will believe in him, and the Romans will come and take away both our land and our nation."

> ...Caiaphas, who was high priest that year, said to them, "You know nothing, nor do you consider that it is better for you that one man should die instead of the people, so that the whole nation may not perish. He did not say this on his own, but since he was high priest for that year, he prophesied that Jesus was going to die for the nation... So from that day on, they planned to kill him. John 11: 47-53

The argument is that bad things happen when too many people believe in Jesus. Our civilization is held back, and the glory of man in all his capacity for achievement is retarded. Ignorance and religion are equated and held to be responsible for man's lack of development.

The origin of this perspective, of course, is man's own ego. When man becomes the measure of all things, as he is in the secular order, God, whether you believe in Him or not, has to be marginalized. He is more marginalized in our culture than any of the minorities we like to point to.

What's more, it can easily be argued that we live in a world that is still trying to kill God, and which justifies this by assigning the prevalence of tragedy to believers. From the beginning of time, this dynamic has been so pervasive we should really recognize it more quickly than we do. Religion, but especially the Judeo-Christian tradition, must be done away with because it is the cause of wars, evil, ignorance, and injustice. The cause is not the corruption in the heart of man, but belief in God! And not the Greek kind of God who sits on top of Mt. Olympus randomly throwing bolts of lightning at his unsuspecting subjects. But a God Who is Father to us, Who is full of mercy, goodness, kindness, Who has made everything for our delight and betterment, and Who loves us with such a crazy love that He has even been willing to die for us. This is the God that we work with might and main to deny and exclude.

What's even crazier is that we tried to definitively destroy Him once. But then He rose, conquering death, all evil in the process, and claiming for us an inheritance that utterly transcends anything that can ever be taken away from us. And what is the reaction? The same as the reaction of the Pharisees to Lazarus. Jesus raised Lazarus from the dead and because so many people came to believe; as a result, the furious response of the Pharisees was: "Let's kill him again!"

Somehow we become bent on destroying the eternal because the eternal intrudes upon our immediate plans. Why we are so interested in preserving our "mess of pottage" over the infinite treasures promised us is one of the strange ironies of our fallen nature. And yet in our attempts to deny and destroy the existence of God's real presence among us, we testify to it at the same time.

As we celebrate with special fervor, amidst the disbelieving "signs" of our times, and solicitous for the salvation of all our brothers and sisters, our hearts catch the new fire of the Easter light that pierces the darkness of doubt hanging over the world in which we live. Jesus has triumphed in Resurrection, in glory and majesty; and within the embrace of Our Blessed Mother, whose singular faith during the Paschal Mystery emboldens us, we hold His light for the world to see until He comes again in glory! Alleluia! He lives no more to die, but lives that all may have eternal life!

Questions for Reflection

1. How often do you think of eternity, and is it a point of reference in your discernment or decision-making?

2. What signs of the times do you see, (both positive and negative)?

3. What does Resurrection teach us about death?

4. What does Resurrection teach us about eternal life?

Saint Mary Magdalene,
help us stay in touch with
the Risen Lord.

FINDING INTIMACY IN THE DESERT

In the depths of our being, we all crave intimacy, connection. We enter the world connected and remarkably well-equipped, even as babies, to draw others into relationship with us. The very first moments of a baby's life have to do with bonding, with cementing fundamental relationships with mother, father, siblings, grandparents, extended family. It happens in a rather mysterious way before a baby has developed verbal language or conscious powers of reasoning. Nonetheless, by his very existence he draws people to himself by something that goes beyond a mere sense of obligation or duty on the part of the adults around him.

Agape, or the unconditional love of God for humankind, is sometimes described as being like the innocent love of an adult for a baby. This is how God loves us!

From the beginning, this being in relationships is so much a part of us, so deep a need, that, by our nature, we are always seeking real relationships, and we suffer deeply when we are deprived of them. This is very much in keeping with our being made in the image and likeness of God Who lives in a communion of Persons and Who desires to share this happiness of a relational life with us.

It is equally true that almost from the beginning, the evil one sets out to disrupt and destroy not just particular relationships but all relationships. He knows that if he succeeds in dividing us from God, we will become divided from others, and divided within ourselves as well. Once God is removed, everything fragments.

Relationships fall apart. This was the strategy of the evil one in the Garden of Eden. This is still his objective in every temptation he sends our way. When one considers the incredible breakdown of marriages and family relationships, it is obvious he excels at this. Yet, it is interesting to note that among couples who regularly pray together, the divorce rate is 1%, a striking contrast to the 50% rate found in society at large. God keeps us together. The evil one tears us apart.

Real relationships are always a threat to the evil one. They have a power in them that defeats him. It is no surprise that they are his central target. He severed himself from his relationship with God, and all that is good. He now seeks to pull everyone else out of that same relationship. And so, there is always hidden, within any temptation, a challenge to our relationship with God and the way we live it, which invariably affects the relationship we have with ourselves and with others. What is presented to us is shown in the guise of a good, but the thrust of it always seeks to disturb or break our relationship with God.

Today, a successful strategy used by the evil one is the lure of "alternative" relationships, perhaps with other people, with nature, with technology, or even with himself, (though it is misleading to speak of the possibility of having a real relationship with the devil since he seeks ultimately, not our good but rather our destruction, and has lies and deceptions without number to accomplish it.) He draws us in countless ways, sometimes through vain curiosities that waste time, through pursuit of base appetites, through legitimate goods such as digital gadgets that end up replacing personal relationships in many people's lives. He falsely suggests that the intimacy and inspiration we crave is more effectively met in these ways than in fidelity to God and our loved ones.

Jesus went into the desert to show us the necessity of immersing ourselves in our relationship with our Father. When we are in deep communion with Him we easily recognize temptation and its core object.

It is intriguing to watch what Jesus does as He is tempted by the devil. He does not debate the truth or lie of Satan's statements, for there is always some truth in temptation. He knows Satan's aim. Jesus hears the suggestion to abuse grace by turning stones into bread, to presume on or test God's love by throwing Himself down from a height (and every fall from grace is exactly that) and to replace worship of God with the worship of Satan in the interests of exalting Himself as ruler of the kingdoms of the world. Jesus responds by defending the Father's ways and holding fast to Him. Real love always recognizes a threat to its treasure and is not moved by self-interest but rather willing to sacrifice self to preserve that treasure.

Jesus shows us that in the desert, in a poverty where we strip ourselves of excess and superfluous things, we much more readily attend to and are able to enter into this living relationship with God. This is what our life is truly about. In the desert, less is more. In the desert we are strengthened, not weakened. In the desert, God can speak to our hearts, as the prophet says (Hosea: 2:14). In the desert, we conquer, with Christ, the evil one who is always looking for ways to take us out.

The traditional practices of Lent: prayer, fasting, and alms-giving have this aim. They are not mere disciplines or exercises of will. They are instruments of healing, meant to strengthen our relationships, especially in areas where we have either been negligent or where the evil one has caused damage. Prayer helps heal and strengthen our relationship with God. Fasting heals the brokenness we have within ourselves, addressing especially our tendencies to selfishness. Giving alms helps to heal the brokenness we have in relation to others.

Holiness is nothing more than this: being in the right relationship with God, with each other, and with ourselves. Lent is a time in which particular grace is given to correct our relationships and bring us to the intimacy with God we are created for. When we come to this kind of holiness then we will have power and protection against evil, joy even in the midst of suffering, and grace-filled effectiveness in whatever God asks us to do in mission and ministry. May this Lent bring us, through the Holy Spirit, to become one with Jesus in His love for the Father, His love for us, and His love for all our brothers and sisters. May Our Lady inflame our desire for this life of love, and especially accompany us and protect us in our efforts.

Questions for Reflection

1. The devil often mixes truth and lies together. We can be tempted to listen to him because of the truth he throws into his deceptions. Jesus shows us that regardless of this, we do not take direction from a creature who was a liar and a murderer from the beginning. Have you ever experienced being led to a bad decision because of something that initially appeared good?

2. What is your relationship with God the Father like? How do you think of Him?

3. What are some of the "alternative" relationships you have been tempted with?

4. What is your response to strong temptations? Do you recognize them when they come as something to be resisted?

Saints Joachim and Anne,
help us stay together.

DESTINY AND THE BLESSING OF FATHERS

Deprivation can be an awful thing. There are many serious poverties in the world today. But there is one poverty that is too easily overlooked and yet produces some of the most far-reaching effects upon destiny that one can imagine. This is the poverty that comes from the lack of a father's blessing.

Scripture shows us from the very beginning of creation that there is a fundamental principle for growth and well-being. This principle is even more necessary in a fallen world. The principle shown to us by God Himself is that if something is to flourish, the good must be correctly recognized and properly blessed. Pure and simple! God's joyful affirmation of the work of His own hands ignites creation's growth and development and multiplies its fruitfulness. Our Heavenly Father blesses our world from its inception.

The fruit of every womb also awaits blessing, a blessing that God has willed should come in a special way from fathers. Without this blessing, even mothers can find it harder to receive their children as gifts from God. (70% of all women who have had abortions cite the father of the child as the primary influence in their decision.)

Without the blessing of fathers, wherein the goodness of each child is personally acknowledged and celebrated, we end up with a society of orphans, children who grow up with a gnawing hunger for acceptance, for an affirmation of their very existence.

Consider the consequences of fatherless homes:

85% of all children who show behavior disorders come from fatherless homes. The absence of a biological father increases by 900 percent a daughter's vulnerability to rape and sexual abuse, and for boys has been linked to sexual maladjustment and greater and greater aggressiveness or exaggerated masculine behavior.

63% of youth suicides are from fatherless homes. 71% of all high school dropouts come from fatherless homes. 90% of all homeless and runaway children are from fatherless homes. 80% of rapists with anger problems come from fatherless homes. 85% of all youths in prison come from fatherless homes. And 70% of youths in State institutions come from homes without fathers.

The United States has the highest rate in the world of children who are not living with their biological fathers (25 million). The wounds created in a child by this are numberless. The fruit of non-blessing causes people to labor under unnecessary weights and burdens that can drag them to despair and eventual destruction. This is not just a psychological principle: It's a profoundly spiritual one!

Today, there are mountains of books written on discipline and parenting. None of these are nearly as important as understanding the power of a father's blessing, presence, and involvement in the life of a child. His role is irreplaceable!

If people want healing in their families, and by extension, in society, they must learn what real blessing is and start blessing. Blessing will stabilize and set the foundations for restoration. Blessing will strengthen and multiply the goodness already present. Cursing and blaspheming, berating, criticizing, and nit-picking, so prevalent today as to often go unnoticed, will bring a house, a family, to ruin in no time.

There is no greater need today than that the hearts of fathers be turned to their children. A child may occasionally abuse his parents' blessing as the prodigal son did, yet it was that father's very blessing that drew him back home and restored him.

There is hope! Malachi prophesied almost 25 centuries ago (3: 23-24):

> Lo, I will send you Elijah, the prophet,
> Before the day of the Lord comes,
> The great and terrible day,
> To turn the hearts of the fathers to their children,
> And the hearts of the children to their fathers,
> Lest I come and strike the land with doom.

Scripture provides the warning, but also the remedy once we have lost the gift. "...A father's blessing strengthens the houses of the children..." (Sirach 3:9), and all creation looks forward to the revelation of the sons of God" (Romans 8:19). All society awaits the peace and order and benefit that will come when fathers truly learn the transforming power of God's love, which is theirs to communicate to their children.

*(see http://firstthings.org/father-facts)

Questions for Reflection

1. How have you experienced fatherhood in your own life?

2. Why do you think so many fathers are missing in action?

3. What will it take to heal fatherhood today?

4. Is there anything women can do to help heal the wounds of the masculine soul?

Saint Joseph, teach manly fathers to be godly fathers.

A PASSING LOOK
AT FOOTBALL

I love football! I come from a family of nine: Mom, Dad, six brothers, and myself. From late August through January, the Sunday family ritual growing up always included football. Packers football. No question. We all went to Mass together, came home, ate a meal together, and then settled in the living room, ready for a good game and a win for our team. We loved being able to throw ourselves into the game with Dad. And he enjoyed teaching us all he knew. As a result, I can talk football with the best of them.

Yet, and this is difficult to admit, my observation today is that football has become a kind of liturgy of the secular culture. And unfortunately, it is the only "liturgy" many people participate in on a weekend.

Consider the typical game. There is a communal gathering, most often on a Sunday. The game begins with an entrance procession in which the specially vested (uniformed) enter the sanctuary (stadium.). An opening hymn (National Anthem) is sung. The seating of the congregation (fans/crowd) takes place, and the beginning of lengthy commentaries (mini homilies) on the gameplay starts. The crowd has the "appropriate" responses before, during and after. And, of course, there is special football food and drink. The homage paid is evidenced by the offering of incredible amounts of time, money, and attention on both sides of the ball, by the management, the team and by the fans, all elements of Liturgy, but without the Divine.

It's salutary to remember that worship and recreation/entertainment are two different things. Archbishop Fulton Sheen pointed out that if we do not worship God, we worship something, and nine times out of ten it will be ourselves.

For as much as we love anything, the truth is that the coin of Caesar is not the currency of heaven. Hollywood stars, sports heroes, and any famous person will not find entrance there based on their popularity, or performance in their field. They may be known the world over, yet still hear The Lord say: "Depart from Me. I never knew you." One of my favorite quarterbacks has said he doesn't think God "cares a whole lot about the outcome of a game. He cares about the people involved." (Aaron Rodgers) As Jesus said: "What does it profit a man if he gain the whole world yet loses his soul." Mark 8:36. The measure of success in this world is hardly the measure of success in the next.

But is there still room for football on a Sunday? I hope so. With a few cautions. Like anything we enjoy, there can be an inclination to go overboard and to give inordinate amounts of attention to what we love until before we know it, it has become a kind of idol.

Yet, it is also true that our attraction to physical and moral excellence touches on our yearning for the transcendent, which will only be completely realized in Christ. He is the fullness of all excellence! That is why excellence is exciting to see in any area. Sports is no exception. St. Pope John Paul II expressed this beautifully:

> ...every sport, at both the amateur and competitive level, requires basic human qualities such as rigorous preparation, continual training, awareness of one's personal limits, fair competition, acceptance of precise rules, respect for one's opponent and a sense of solidarity and unselfishness...When sports are played and understood in the right way, they are an extraordinary expression of a person's best

inner energies and of his ability to overcome difficulties, to set goals to be reached through sacrifice, generosity, and determination in facing the difficulties of competition.

These are all lessons to be learned and disciplines to be cultivated in facing the ever-present challenges and battles that need to be won in our own everyday lives. We compete, we run the race, we fight the good fight, that we may attain the one prize that is everlasting!

Questions for Reflection

1. Why is it so easy to become obsessed with sports and sports stars? Do you see any danger signs in your own involvement with sports?

2. Do you recognize any other idols in your life?

3. How much time do you spend with God in the course of a week?

4. What do you spend the most time on when you are not working?

5. What do you need to do to free yourself from the pull of inordinate attachments?

Pope Saint John Paul II,
with Saint Sebastian,
Patron of Athletes,
grant us the grace to make
the sports we watch and play
a winning way to praise and pray.

COME LORD JESUS
(Advent Thoughts)

t this time when **Mary and Joseph are following an inner vision, the three Kings are following** an extraordinary star, and angels are appearing to shepherds near Bethlehem, we too turn the eyes of our souls toward the great Gift that comes to us in the Person of Jesus, our Savior.

We may think this is old news: that Jesus comes to save us. But it seems that in the world today, the same world that lay in darkness at the Advent of Christ's birth, we have need of a greater appreciation of our need to be saved.

Man has tried over the ages to save himself. And though often well-intentioned, the simple truth persists: "if the Lord does not build the house, in vain do the builders labor." –Ps 127:1

We often live our lives without ever really seeking the whole salvation that Jesus comes to give us. He not only wants to free us from sin, but from worry, from resentment, from wounds and hurts that keep us bound to the past, from loneliness, from narrowness, from boredom, from indifference, from blindness, from selfishness, from our suspicions, our doubts, our negativity and fears, from self-sufficiency, from everything that leads us to spiritual starvation. He comes to give us life, and the more abundant life!

Yet how often do we use our words to try and save ourselves or others, instead of going to the Word to be saved by it. Or how often do we think **our work, our apostolate, our service** is the vehicle of salvation, forgetting that the work belongs to God and will only be made fruitful in Him.

We form human alliances instead of striving to live in communion with the Triune God, who gives, heals and elevates every relationship. Or we stand in judgment over others rather than loving them and escaping our own judgment by living God's charity, which He promises covers a multitude of sins.

We try to save ourselves from our addictions and only end up replacing one with another. We do the same with our weaknesses. We spiritualize them in an attempt to still our consciences rather than seeking and depending upon God's merciful grace. Our real self, which we hide, nevertheless dogs us into our life of prayer and charity toward our neighbor, especially those we live with. So we try to heal our brokenness with all sorts of self-help programs instead of letting God help us.

Jesus knows how hard it is for us to acknowledge our need to be saved. He knows how our pride blinds us. He knows how  difficult it is for us to approach Him unguardedly. So He comes to us as a tiny baby, and as babies are able to do, draws us to Himself and commands our attention and affection by His beauty and littleness. There is no other human being we take as quickly to ourselves as a little baby. There is no other that disarms us and wins our hearts and our affections so quickly. There is no other creature that draws the good from within us, all that is human, the way a baby does, and most importantly, the way the Baby Jesus does.

May each of us this Christmas be given, and receive in all humility, the eyes of the Shepherds, the determination of the Wise Men to follow the vision of the Star, and the heart and soul of Mary and Joseph who so eagerly saw and so completely received the magnificent love come to us Incarnate in Christ Jesus our little Lord and mighty Savior.

Come Lord Jesus. Come to save us! Do not delay!

Questions for Reflection

1. What parts of your life do you keep to yourself and away from Jesus?

2. What part do you think shame plays in self-sufficiency?

3. How does Jesus help you conquer yourself so you can draw near to Him?

4. Which figures in the Nativity story do you identify with the most?

Blessed Anna Maria Taigi, patroness of mothers
and Saint Philomena, patroness of infants,
help us to become like little children
so we can join you in heaven.

A WORD REGARDING
THE REAL WAR ON WOMEN

ecently PBS aired a documentary on women in 6 different countries called *Half the Sky*, based on the book of the same name, by Nicholas Kristof and his wife, Sheryl WuDunn.

Countries featured in the documentary were: Sierra Leone, where rape as a weapon of choice during the civil war there has now become mainstream; Cambodia, where sex-trafficking brothels are filled with younger and younger girls who are locked up and even caged, made to take "clients" non-stop; Vietnam, where girls, especially from the countryside, are discriminated out of educations and left with little hope for much of a future; Somaliland, where genital mutilation still goes on, causing chronic pain and complications, and where a considerable percentage of women die in childbirth because of these complications and the lack of medical care; India, where the caste system and dire poverty still creates a conducive environment for parents to sell their young girls into brothels, traumatizing them for life, and where generational prostitution is an entrenched way of life for many women; Kenya, where violence against women is so prevalent that women have begun initiatives of education and microfinance to begin to bring change to their situations.

And then there's China, which wasn't mentioned, with its one-child policy that has resulted in forced abortions, sterilizations, infanticide (of girls) and a huge gender imbalance that creates fertile ground for human trafficking.

There's another country where women have been victimized by a powerful propaganda that has brought them to be ashamed of their bodies and the meaning of their bodies. Because of this propaganda, they have sterilized themselves in great numbers and had 50 million of their babies killed in the last 40 years.

All this has been done under a euphemism called "women's reproductive health." How it is exactly that women's healthcare becomes synonymous with ending newly conceived life and disabling reproductive capacity, is the unasked question. But the underlying falsehood is that women can't be equal to men unless 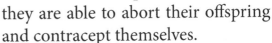 they are able to abort their offspring and contracept themselves.

This country, of course, is the United States of America; and many countries in the West now promote this propaganda. The hidden lie is that women cannot have control of their destiny unless they can get rid of what actually makes them women. So they must have free access to abortion, contraception, and sterilization.

People say this is a non-issue in our society and culture, that there is no real war against women in this country. Yet, if we don't get this fundamental question right, everything else is skewed. The question of how we understand woman is a question of primary importance because it affects one half of our population and how that population participates in bringing this country to true greatness.

Make no mistake about this. The current propaganda has been just as lethal to women and children in the US as anything that goes on in any country in Asia or Africa or Latin America. Any man (or woman) who encourages a woman to think that access to contraception, sterilization, and abortion will make her equal to men has rejected her womanhood and therefore has rejected her as a real person. Are there injustices against women? Of course. Are their things that need to change? Of course. Do women need support in times of crisis and difficulty? Without question. But is this the best answer we are able to come up with?

In the countries mentioned above, incredible, selfless people, many of them victims themselves, are doing tremendous outreach and helping to change things. They are women (and men) of real courage. They are fighting to bring about real change, raising the standard of women's lives to what they should be. Some of the answers will need to be rethought. But the positive movement is there. As the documentary says: "Women and girls are part of the solution, not the problem."

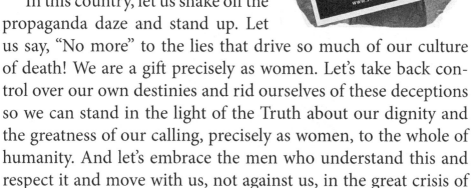

In this country, let us shake off the propaganda daze and stand up. Let us say, "No more" to the lies that drive so much of our culture of death! We are a gift precisely as women. Let's take back control over our own destinies and rid ourselves of these deceptions so we can stand in the light of the Truth about our dignity and the greatness of our calling, precisely as women, to the whole of humanity. And let's embrace the men who understand this and respect it and move with us, not against us, in the great crisis of this hour!

For women who have been used and deceived by this present culture, take heart! The good news is that the truth, even when painful, really does set us free. Real change begins in the heart. And women are creatures of the heart. Once we realize the deception that has been foisted upon us, the lies that have been used for our own destruction can be stripped of their power, and the feminine genius can then be unleashed for the building up of a genuine civilization of life and love.

Questions for Reflection

1. What lies do you recognize in the culture today and what has been the fruit of those lies?

2. What do you think is necessary to change our culture from a culture of death to a civilization of life and love?

3. In the face of grave moral crises, what causes the apathy we see?

4. What does the Holy Spirit offer us to remedy the deep confusions of our day?

Saint Josphine Bakhita,
plead mercy for the violent and their victims.

UNDERSTANDING THE STORY OF OUR LIVES
A LENTEN REFLECTION

It is a positive fact that one day, all of us will leave the **bounds of time** and enter into the limitless realms of eternity. The light of heaven will reveal to us things that eye has not seen, ear has not heard, and the mind of man has not conceived.

But while we live in time our lives are probably best characterized by the kind of story they tell, or, have begun to tell. They can be small stories or great stories, subplots that weave in and out of greater narratives. The beauty of a story is that it develops over time. And while it is yet being written, the plot evolves, characters change, conflicts surface, challenges are faced, good and evil wrestle, heroes are born, villains are conquered, and new adventures are begun. Heroes may fall. But even if they fall many times yet rise again to greatness, our hearts thrill just as they do when villains are converted. Until the last chapter is written, suspense works in us, and hope keeps vigil while we strain to the greatness we are created to live.

Every person's life is really a unique story, one which can be read in different ways. A life can be understood in the context of family or of an even greater history, whether that be a history of the Church or the world, or God's ongoing relationship with man in creation, salvation, and glory.

Jesus' life has been called: "The Greatest Story Ever Told," and our life story becomes especially exciting when we begin to see and understand it in the light of Jesus' own life. Our life then becomes another story of God's infinite and unwearied love for us. At the same time, God's love gives to the story of our lives a participation in His own Life, and a special work, a mission we alone can fully accomplish. Part of the adventure of living is discovering our unique mission and playing out our beautiful and irreplaceable role in the much greater drama of God's undying love for humanity.

This drama is the Lord's, but it is ours too. It is divine but human also, a mingling of splendid creatures made from ash and mud, living in communion with angels and saints whose respective worlds, heaven and earth, the flesh and the spirit, interpenetrate each other even now.

We are all meant to be unique heroes in this great epic. The saints are true heroes, and we are called to this same heroism, a heroism that has as many possible expressions as there are people born into the world, because it can only be lived and expressed in a personal way, in our particular relationship with God.

There is no real narrative thread outside God, nothing with the power to give meaning, to unify and integrate the complexities of the human heart or explain the struggles and yearnings that inhabit the depths of a soul and that steer the course of our history, our story as a people. Man tends toward God by His very nature. And this will always lead him outside himself in a quest to be a part of something greater, something transformative and transcendent. The awakening of a living Faith in our lives draws us into a real adventure with the Triune God, with our loving and provident Father, with Jesus our Savior and Brother, and with the Holy Spirit, our Comforter and Guide. They fill our lives, our stories, with the best of all characters, a Mother like no other, and brothers and sisters who surround us with unending help.

When time shall be no more, this drama of Faith, written in the great voluminous Book of Life, will be read in heaven over and over again to the delight of its citizens. All will have played an important role, whether obvious or hidden, in the grand story that ends in the triumphant victories of Christ and the communion of God with man for all eternity.

Shakespeare said: "It is not in the stars to hold our destiny but in ourselves." Lent is a time to sharpen the focus of our life narrative. It is a time to take the editor's pen to the bad ideas, the bad habits, the bad attitudes, the bad writing, that makes us mediocre or worse. It is a time to strengthen the character of the hero that lives in us, and to come into conformity with the life of the greatest Hero ever (Christ), by aligning our lives more closely to His and adopting His Spirit in the vicissitudes of life, whether they be joyful, sorrowful, luminous or glorious. We must always be aware that the course of our story, our life, will, in turn, affect the course of countless other stories, lives that interface with ours, for better or for worse.

The Book of Revelation gives us a glimpse of the end of time:

Then I saw a great white throne and Him Who sat upon it; from His presence earth and sky fled away and no place was found for them. And I saw the dead, great and small, standing before the throne, and books were opened. Also another book was opened, which is the book of life. And the dead were judged by what was written in the books, by what they had done. Rev. 20: 11:15

May our Lenten exercises during this Year of Faith, become a source of grace for some of the greatest chapters of our lives, masterpieces in their witness to the great mystery of God's love for mankind.

(Inspired by William Kilpatrick's *Life is a Story*, chapter
from *Why Johnny Can't Tell Right From Wrong*.)

Questions for Reflection

1. What similarities do you find in your own life to the life of Jesus?

2. What does Jesus' life teach you about your own life?

3. What role are you currently playing in your life story? Are you actively engaged or are you more of a passive bystander, watching your life just happen?

4. At the end of your life, what title would you like your life story to have?

Saint Mary Helen MacKillop,
encourage us to grow into the persons
Jesus wants us to become.

THE SPIRIT OF HEROD AND THE INNOCENCE OF THE LAMB

his December 14, 2012, the spirit of Herod brutally intruded upon our world, upon a people in festive excitement and preparation for Christmas, many anticipating the birth of Our Savior and King. In a little town in Connecticut, at a grade school where the approach of Christmas gave the children there special light and anticipation, twenty children and six adults trying to protect them were suddenly and mercilessly gunned down for no discernible reason. Just as the death of the Holy Innocents in Jesus' time must surely have in-

volved the death of adults, mothers and fathers desperate to save the lives of their children, so in Newtown, 6 adults gave their lives to do the same.

Jesus comes into our darkness this Christmas, into a world shocked by its own violence and yet blinded to some of the deepest violence embedded now in its own way of life. A question perennially present once again breaks through the surface into our anguish to demand an answer: Where does this violence come from? Is it situational? Is it cultural? Is there a hereditary predisposition to it? Why does this keep happening?

This problem reveals itself at the beginning of time when Cain first raised his hand and spilled the blood of his own brother. It comes down to a simple premise. What rules our lives! There are only two answers here. We choose self-rule, or we allow God to order our lives according to His wisdom.

Our first parents chose self-rule and left us the inheritance of that choice: shattered relationships, disharmony, weakness, toil, excessive self-love, the loss of divine gifts, a tendency to be enslaved by sin, the flesh, evil, violence and finally, death.

This is a choice we all make. We choose either self-rule or God's wisdom, God's way. This is a choice we must make as a people as well. And our choice will determine our future.

History shows that self-rule is a seedbed for many tragedies. The first to suffer under the tyranny of self-rule? The weakest, most vulnerable and innocent: the unborn, children, the disabled, the elderly, the poor. All those who cannot defend themselves against the lust for self-seeking power that self-rule generates in man's soul are at risk. (Note: the use of the term self-rule here signifies something different than self-control or self-mastery.)

At the same time, those we marginalize are a reflection of the greatest marginalization of all — God. God is the most marginalized Person in our world today. We push Him out of public life, our government, our schools, out of our personal lives, and now there is even an attempt to regulate God in the confines of His own House, telling Him He must be subject to the government in His dictates to us. (see HHS mandate)

This is a marginalization that began with the Fall and is perpetuated every time we choose ourselves over Love. We live in a society that has chosen again and again to proclaim self-rule over God's wisdom. And this is deadly. Self-rule as a principle for a people will always degenerate into barbarism, for self-rule, infected as it is by selfishness, rarely is able to exert itself in the discipline of Christian virtue. It is unable because the practice of virtue requires denying oneself for a greater good, a good beyond self.

Jesus shows us how to choose Love as the rule for ourselves this Christmas, even in our deepest darknesses. He shows us how to choose Him by His example of continually choosing us, no matter the level of depravity we sink to. The witness of the children and teachers slain in Sandy Hook is a witness of this kind

of love: innocent love in the children and its mature counterpart, self-giving love in the adults. If we want more adults who are self-giving, one thing is certain, we have to stop destroying the innocence of our children.

This kind of love is the only thing capable of conquering the separation, isolation, selfishness, and violence that is born of our narcissistic self-rule. Our hope and our faith reside in the Gift that comes to us this Christmas, that precisely in our deepest darknesses and even though we marginalize Him to the stable, God comes, He still comes to us...in the pure, selfless, innocent love of a Baby Who hides within Himself the glory of the Divinity's desire to save us, to heal us, to take away our tears, to restore our hearts and to gladden us with His presence.

Mary knows what Her child is destined for; she receives the prophecy of the sword that hangs over her own heart. But She also knows the victory that Her Son, Love Incarnate, is destined to win. Her faith holds us fast while in the dangers and evils and violence of the present age, the darkness is surely and definitively being banished away.

We mourn with the families of Newtown, like Rachel mourning her children because they are no more, though we know they are safe now with the Lord. But we know too with firm conviction, and without passing judgment, that the spirit of Herod, Herod whose self-indulgence led him to madness and a worm-eaten end, is vanquished by the love of the innocent Child whose promise of a restored inheritance is ours if we have the wisdom to choose it, an inheritance where:

> ...the lowly will ever find joy in the Lord...for the tyrant will be no more, and the arrogant will have gone, and all who are alert to do evil will be cut off. Isaiah 29: 19-20

Questions for Reflection

1. What do you observe of the attack upon innocence in the world today? What generates it?

2. In the battle between the kingdoms of light and darkness, how does the light conquer? Is there evidence today of the light of Christ conquering evil?

3. If the source of evil acts comes from the heart, what is necessary to heal the heart of so many today who commit these senseless acts?

4. Do you see any signs of narcissism in yourself? Try to be honest with yourself.

Holy child martyrs
St. Jose Santos del Rio
and Antonio Molla Lazo,
grant courage
and protection
to the innocent
threatened by attacks
of murderous hatred.

GIVING UP SECRETS

Our age is an age of secrets. **Governments, corporations, educational, medical, and religious institutions** are all skilled at keeping secrets both for good reasons and not so good reasons. Media definitely keeps secrets according to the agenda it pushes. But this reflects people in general. People tend to keep a lot of secrets.

There is a pressing need to recognize that secrets make a difference. They can determine the direction of our lives, and the manner in which we pass from this world into the next. Few of us can admit to being ready for heaven when we consider that in heaven, our insides will show on the outside. Nothing will be hidden. Everything will be transparent.

Jesus tells us in the Gospels that everything that is hidden now will be revealed. Secret activities, secret wounds, secret weaknesses, secret sins, secret fantasies, secret thoughts, secret addictions, secret jealousies, secret plans, secret ambitions, family secrets, secret judgments, secret desires, in fact, a secret life, all of it will be revealed. That is unless you have taken care of any sin in your secrets, by going to Confession where God annihilates the sin and wills to remember it no more. Then they will never be brought up as a testimony against you.

Ironically, we hide things about ourselves but at the same time, have an attraction to know the secrets of others. There is almost nothing people like better than hearing a good secret. Why? There are several reasons. One, it diverts attention away from our own secrets. But we also love secrets because we love hidden knowledge. We live in a state of being that is still looking for something that hasn't been completely revealed to us yet. We're searching, whether we know it or not, for the one Word that will answer all of our questions and give sight to the vision, the understanding we seek.

The devil knows this about us. Would that people understood that the devil has to penetrate the world of knowledge by study and observation too (albeit with a superior intelligence,) and that he perverts what he knows to his own ends. Those ends are not full of happy consequences for human souls.

He is interested in luring people away from the real light. He does it with promises of hidden knowledge, just as he did in the Garden of Eden. (This is also one of the most lucrative marketing techniques around. Money rolls in when you claim to have the secret to long life, to health, to beauty, to happiness, to success. This is also one of the reasons professional gossips, psychics, and clairvoyants prosper in our culture today. People want to know those secrets.)

We, on the other hand, have the source of all knowledge, the fount of pure Wisdom and Light in God Himself. And we have  been given, in Jesus Christ, and through His Church, a direct line to that source, Who is for us, our true Father (the Father of all lights). The temptations of some dark meddler should never cause us to turn our glance away from our Good Father, as our first parents did in the Garden, and as we so often do in our own lives.

Interestingly enough, Jesus mentions that the Father Himself keeps secrets from the "wise and learned" and reveals things to the "little ones." Why is that? (This might have been a good question for Adam and Eve to have asked as they were being tempted to eat of the tree of the knowledge of good and evil.) We know most certainly that God never does anything without good reason, and a reason that redounds, often in mysterious ways, to our greatest benefit.

Might it be that God protects the sacred and hides divine treasures for our sake? Anyone who has studied the covenant knows that profaning the sacred is dangerous. We can be destroyed by our profanation. A simple look at the human wreckage surrounding the modern desecration of the gift and mystery of sexuality confirms this.

In other words, could it be that just as Jesus told us not to cast pearls before swine, He follows His own counsel with us? He puts His treasure in safe places. He is careful with what is precious beyond measure. And at the same time, He is merciful to those of us who would have a terrible accounting to give for squandering a poorly understood gift if we received it and did not appreciate or care for it.

Secrets like this can be a good thing; they can be a very good thing if their purpose is to protect a treasure (whether that be jewels or a reputation) from vandalism or theft, misuse or destruction.

But some secrets should never be kept. And unfortunately, people usually have more of these kinds of secrets.

We pay a price for many of the secrets we keep. We can safely say, I think, that many of the sicknesses of our age are determined by the secrets we keep. This is well known in the world of addiction and co-dependency: "We are only as sick as our secrets." This is actually a psychology that was first explicated in the Sacred Scriptures. Psalm 32 says: "I kept it secret and my frame was wasted…" The distress, the groaning, the anxiety, the depression, the disturbance of so many today more often than not comes from holding secrets that should not be kept.

St. Paul mentions this relationship between spiritual realities and physical consequences. He says, in 1Corinthians, 11:29:

> For anyone who eats and drinks without recognizing the body of the Lord eats and drinks judgment on himself. That is why many among you are weak and sick, and a number of you have fallen asleep.

With the rising tide of illnesses in our age, we await a physician who will make this connection and diagnose the real cause of so many of the physical and psychological disorders of our day.

I know a woman who struggled with terrible depression much of her adult life, watched Mother Angelica faithfully, but would not take the secret of her abortion to the Confessional. She died recently, and my prayer is that before she died she finally released her secret into the loving mercy of God so she could enter her heavenly home with "joy and an upright heart." Her secret certainly didn't keep her in peace or bring happiness into her life. It brought her to the verge of a mental breakdown. So why do we keep the secrets we do? This is a mystery, really, since we only fool ourselves in keeping these kinds of secrets. God is certainly not fooled. There is nothing He doesn't know about us. The story of Ananias and Sapphira, found in the fifth chapter of Acts, tells us exactly what can happen when we dissemble before God. They pretended (to the Lord, as St. Peter points out) that they were giving everything to the community of believers, when in fact they retained a portion for themselves which they could have rightfully retained if they had chosen to. After St. Peter had spoken, Ananias, and later his wife Sapphira (who arrived late and was ques-

tioned separately) both died on the spot, apparently for attempting to deceive God.

Keeping secrets from God is impossible, and it can be deadly! If not immediately, then at our own judgments, when in our encounter with God Who is pure Love and Light and Goodness, all that is hidden will be revealed. To our overwhelming confusion we will find ourselves suddenly naked before the Lord, rather than clothed in the garments of grace He so freely and continually offers us, all because fear, or attachment or pride kept us from giving up our secrets.

Does this mean we should blurt out everything to everyone all the time like they do on the tacky talk shows that seem to pollute the airwaves? No. There is something inherently debasing about psychologically disrobing in front of millions of people. There is something degrading about vomiting up things in public that properly belong in a counselor's office and more often in a Confessional where the justification, relief, and redemption that people are seeking can really be given.

This is really how Saints begin to become Saints. They get rid of their secrets. And they don't lie to themselves about who they really are. That is why they are such shining examples of humility. They know themselves in Truth, and it sets them free to soar to the heights! They give their secrets, both their sins and their treasures, over to God. He takes the sins, and in Confession completely annihilates them, wills to remember them no more. They are gone, gone, gone, with no more power to determine their life, and will never again reappear in accusation against them, even at the end of time. Never!

And then our Father does an even more astounding thing. He begins giving them "treasures out of the darkness and riches that have been hidden away." Isaiah 45:3 He takes miserable secrets and begins to replace them with the secrets He holds. What an exchange! The saints are no fools! They know this bargain is unmatched anywhere in the whole universe. In the heart of our Redeemer, we are given, by way of His own sacrificial love, infinite riches in exchange for giving to Him our sinfulness, our pride, our imperfections, our self-importance.

Great Confessors, like St. John Vianney and St. Padre Pio spent themselves in this work of getting people to give up their secrets so that they could begin to know the deep things of God in their lives. There is a reason the sacrament of Peace and Reconciliation is an Easter Sacrament. There is a reason that the Holy Spirit, Who comes in Pentecost like a mighty wind to sweep out the secret and dark recesses of our souls and fill them with fire and light, is the culminating gift of the Easter season.

Our Blessed Mother, the most pure creature who ever lived, was without secrets of her own. She kept only those God gave her. And because of that, there is no one more beautiful, more radiantly transparent in the living of the Mysteries of the Most Holy Trinity. In Her many apparitions in the last centuries, we can hear the cry of our good Mother when she bids us return to the Sacraments and live the Gospel way of life. One of the things She is saying with great affection and urgency, as if speaking to a little child, is: "Run! Run and whisper your secrets to your Father. All of them! And be assured that He will give treasures out of the darkness and riches that have been hidden away especially for you!"

Questions for Reflection

1. What is your experience of secrets?

2. Families that are unhealthy often keep secrets that block the possibility of healing. Children then learn to hide things, especially observations and feelings. Jesus often begins surfacing things in us, bringing them to our consciousness, bringing them out into the light so that healing can happen. Yet, people resist this. Why?

3. What is the real purpose of a secret? How can it help? How can it harm?

4. Do you have any secrets you wish you didn't have? What would you need to do to be freed from that burden?

Saint Margaret Clitherow,
when the secret was told that you were hiding priests
in secret rooms in your house, you and the child hiding in your
womb were slowly crushed to death by the secret police.
That you loved Jesus more than life was a secret you could not keep.

THE HEALING POWER OF SILENCE

e live in a wilderness, a wilderness of noise. Noise is not just about sound. It has to do with the constant barrage of stimulation to our senses, emotions, and even our intellect (read information overload.) The problem with all this noise, pure and simple, is that it is an obstacle to our own inner order and peace, and more importantly, to a living communion with God and with others.

For some reason, many of us seem afraid of silence or, more likely; we have lost familiarity with the wonders of silence. Yet it is essential to our physical and spiritual well-being. Authentic silence is not emptiness. Things come to us in the silence. We hear new languages. We are visited by penetrating peace, insight, God Himself, His wisdom, light, His perception, and understanding. In authentic silence, we hear new sounds and enter new worlds. In silence we come to know our own hearts.

It is interesting to note how often people observe that the sounds God has put in creation: wind rustling in the trees, birds chirping, the lapping of waves at the ocean, are a balm to the soul. This stands in stark contrast to the agitation and disturbance created by the sounds of the modern world driven by mechanical energy and a volume, a pitch that does violence to one's nerves, stressing them beyond what they are meant to endure. Silence is almost completely exiled from our modern culture. Yet it is exceedingly important for us.

Silence, in fact, is so important to us that it may be one of the main reasons God has structured us to sleep a third of our days. We know that when we can't sleep, when our bodies and minds are deprived of the stillness good sleep brings, we become sick. Anyone who struggles with insomnia knows the anxiety and frustration lack of sleep brings. "If I could just sleep, I would feel better," is the all too common cry. For those saints who were able to pray the night away and not be ill-affected, it was because they entered a deep contemplative silence that so rejuvenated soul and spirit, the body was refreshed and strengthened by it…

In the Liturgy, given to us by God through Moses on Mt Sinai, and Jesus at the Last Supper, there are spaces for silence. That tells us that silence is part of a Divine Rhythm, part of the rhythm of life in Heaven…it tells us silence is a good thing, a medium for God's communication of Himself to us. The lives of Jesus, Mary, and St. Joseph, in particular, bear striking witness to the insepa-rability of silence from great holiness.

In those who are progress-ing in prayer, in the inner expe-rience of the presence of God, silence becomes a medium for God's deeper and deeper com-munication of Himself to the soul. St. Teresa calls one of the early stages of contemplative prayer, the Prayer of Quiet. God begins to suspend, or silence or still the human activity of the mind, the will, the memory, the imagination, the passions, so that He can communicate Himself more deeply. And in that, the soul itself begins to be healed of its defects and weaknesses and disor-der. St. John of the Cross poetically describes this as: "My house being now all stilled…" He goes on to say that once there is this stillness (which comes through real purifications) the soul is now able to go out to find God without hindrance or distraction. This, by the way, is often something one sees in those who are going through the process of dying. They become strangely quiet in the

months and weeks preceding their deaths. It is as if they no lon-
ger have words. In the activity
of God in their souls, as they
are being readied to enter eternity, they often go through, all
at once, the purifications as
well as the sweet visitations of
the Lord, that the person who
prays regularly, goes through
over a period of time.

We are all interested in healing these days. This is the true
healing we seek, that which comes to us from God Himself, the
Divine Physician, and which heals us from the inside out and orders our inner being to bring it into communion with He Who is
our ultimate bliss and fulfillment.

If we want to be healthy, we must cultivate spaces of silence in
our lives. Not the isolating silence so many live in, but a silence
that nurtures peace within and communion without. One place
to begin is to keep our Churches as sanctuaries of silence, not
places for chit chat.

Another concrete step is to set aside real-time for silence. Silent prayer. Not vocal prayer but a prayer of presence, of being,
in silence, in the presence of the Lord, even for 5 minutes a day,
preferably in a place where there is no outside noise. (That may be
early in the morning before the rest of the family rises.) Ask the
Lord to take you into Himself for 5 minutes, to be still and know
that He is God.

Over 100 years ago, Maria Montessori noted that children
have an innate need for intervals of stillness and silence, silence
for her, meaning the cessation of every movement:

> One day, I came into class holding in my arms a baby four
> months old, which I had taken from the arms of its moth-
> er in the courtyard. ... The silence of the little creature

struck me, and I wanted the children to share my feeling. ... To my amazement, I saw an extraordinary tension in the children who watched me. It seemed as though they were hanging on my lips and felt deeply all I was saying. "Then it's breathing," I went on, "how soft it is. None of you could breathe as it does, without making a sound..." The children, surprised and motionless, held their breath. In that moment there was an extraordinary silence; the tick of the clock, which generally could not be heard, became perceptible. It seemed as if the baby had brought with it an atmosphere of silence such as does not exist in ordinary life. This was because no one was making the smallest movement. And from this came the wish to listen to the silence, and hence to reproduce it.

Maria Montessori, *The Secret of Childhood*

She created the "Silence Game" in which children begin practicing this kind of silence for small intervals at first (even 30 seconds), and then for longer periods. There is a joy the children, (and the teacher) experience when they are able to do this. They later come to ask for the Silence Game when things become chaotic or noisy, recognizing that this silence has the power to restore their inner peace and equilibrium. Then, as a year progresses, the silence begins to happen spontaneously, within the whole group. The children will look up when this happens, smile, and go back to their work. The natural, contemplative spirit of the child, over time, is released.

It may seem like passivity to focus on silence when the world is screaming for answers and actions to address its many grave problems. Yet, "if The Lord does not build the house, in vain do he builders labor." Likewise, the walls of Jericho would never have come tumbling down, nor would the people have persisted in the right action if they had not consulted and stayed faithful to the Lord's rather odd directions.

It has become an almost urgent necessity today, to ask Our Lord and Our Lady to lead each of us to the kind of silence we speak of. The release of a true contemplative spirit among us, one in which the Lord lives and moves us, will, in the end, be the key to the salvation of our modern world.

Questions for Reflection

1. How much silence is incorporated into your day?

2. How does silence affect your spirit? Do you become peaceful and still? Or does it cause agitation and anxiety in you, and why?

3. Silence seems to be something that is an essential need. Why would that be? What really happens when we take time in genuine silence?

4. Silence can be appropriate or inappropriate at certain times. What has been your experience with both?

Saint Thomas Aquinas,
lifted to the heights of contemplation,
you finally hushed all your eloquence,
deeming your learned words
mere strands of straw.
Teach us to accept the grace
of quiet listening.

INSIDE THE "ME" VORTEX

ome time ago, CNN reported that a woman named Nadine Schweigert (ND) married herself in a commitment ceremony where she exchanged rings with her "inner groom." There was an actual gathering of family and friends who were encouraged to "blow kisses to the world." One can imagine the theme song of her wedding with a slight variation: *Nobody Loves Me Like I Do.*

Schweigert had been through a painful divorce in which her

two children opted to live with her ex-husband. She drank, smoked, and was 50 pounds overweight, according to her own testimony. At the suggestion of a friend, she married herself, and now feels "happy, joyous, empowered." She says she has come a long way from where she was. She now takes herself on dates, in order "to invest in this relationship."

We might ask what is going on here. Is it pure narcissism? Or is something else at work? The surprising thing is that with a bit of honest examination, we might have to admit that the only difference between Nadine and ourselves is that we haven't thrown ourselves a wedding party. How many of us are married to our own opinions, our own thoughts, our own routines, our own preferences, likes, dislikes, ways of doing things? She simply made visible what many of us live.

At the same time that Nadine arrived at this solution to her unhappiness, more and more young people come to a different kind of resolution: suicide. Almost nothing is more distressing than hearing that another young person has taken their life. It always elicits shock and dismay. How many times do family and friends say they never saw it coming? The son or daughter, sister, brother, friend, had such a promising life ahead of them, and so many people who loved them.

Why is the incidence of young suicides increasing? Why do so few young people really seem to have the joy of their youth anymore? These are questions we must answer. Back in the 13th century, St. Thomas Aquinas stated categorically that man cannot live without joy. He cannot live without joy! When he is deprived of true spiritual joys he will necessarily become addicted to carnal pleasures.

We are not living in a society or culture that knows what true joy is. And we are dying in myriad ways because of it. Addictions of one kind or another have to be the most prevalent affliction of the modern age. And it is a spiritual problem. Addictions lead to obsession, compulsion, depression, sadness, enslavement. These temporary joys not only don't touch the soul, but harm it, bind it, strangle it.

Perhaps the false bravado of many youth today is an armor against some of the most profound insecurity the young have ever had to face. Maybe it is harder than we think for a young person to believe that he is unconditionally wanted and loved; that he is a source of deep joy to his own family when contraception and abortion are so freely used, so prevalent even in their own families; when an addiction of one kind or another takes precedence over his own needs or welfare; when the self- interest of parents and the adults around him eclipse all else. Perhaps he cannot see how his life has unique meaning when it could be as much a matter of chance as a roll of the dice. Maybe he cannot understand how he can be genuinely connected to anything when there seem to be no absolute relationships in his life, nothing he can depend on to be there, no sacrificial love that will reveal him to himself from the outside. One wonders what the psychological effect must be as he watches "adults" not only sterilize themselves but all creation for their own selfish reasons.

Relationally we no longer have set constellations in our lives. There is less and less order in the universe of our interpersonal lives, fewer predictable rotations or orbits. The universe of relationships in many lives changes before one can even map the constellations. That is the experience of young people today. No center of gravity. No orderly solar system. Just free-flying, random bits of mass crashing into other bits of mass, knocking orbits and axes off.

Perhaps youth experience more quickly that the direction of our culture leads nowhere. Its movement does not solidify into anything stable. It spins into self-destruction.

It took humanity centuries to understand the earth was not the center of the universe and that the sun did not revolve around us but rather we around the sun. Scientists tell us that life on earth flourishes because of how we orbit the sun. If the orbit were a fraction off, the planet would quickly become incapable of sustaining life. Likewise, if our personal orbit is around ourselves, or in our self-centeredness, we think everything else revolves around us, we become like an earth spinning on its axis in nothingness, with no warmth or light or atmosphere to sustain us, only cold blackness surrounding us.

We have to come to an understanding of our individual lives. Just as the natural world has centers of gravity, some stronger than others, so too do our lives have forces at work that move us toward or away from life, true life. We need a center of gravity to hold the movements in balance.

If Jesus is our center of gravity and we understand Him as the center around whom we both spin and revolve, we begin to coalesce, to be defined; we become integrated. We come to understand who we are and how we are related to everyone and everything else. Our world makes sense and is guided by very real rules of existence. If we are knocked out of that orbit, if our center is off, or non- existent, we have grave trouble. We spin off by ourselves, into fragments of what we should be and out of relationship to all the other bodies orbiting the true center.

There is in this, also, an answer to our existential need for joy. Pope Benedict says that real joy comes from friendship with God. Is this really possible? Jesus draws us to Himself and calls us friends. How many saints attest to the fact that friendship with God is not only possible; it's a deep need. It's absolutely real, and in fact, the thing that centers us and holds us together. Jesus is a real Person, and He wants us to relate to Him that way. The Father is a real Person and He too wants us to relate to Him that way. The Holy Spirit is a real Person Who also wants us to relate to Him. The Heavens are filled with these relationships, from Mary to the communion of saints to the angelic hosts. They all have a living relationship with us and long for it to be mutual.

We live in an age where the whole world has been knocked out of its true orbit. We are disintegrating, breaking apart, turning into ots of individual vortexes swirling about with greater or lesser force and causing unprecedented damage to everyone around us because self-centeredness creates in us this vortex which makes us small, narrow, unable to embrace people or things around us without harming or destroying them.

Nadine said she was waiting for someone to come along and make her happy. (Perhaps her husband was too busy swirling inside his own vortex.) She must have decided that no one was coming and that she had to do that for herself. One wishes they could warn her that ultimately this will not work either. We just aren't fashioned that way. An exclusive relationship with oneself has no place to go. At the center of it is a great, gnawing loneliness, like a

black hole. "It is not good for man to be alone." If you try to save yourself, you implode, you self-destruct, you lose yourself. It seems with the rise of super-storms, multiple tornadoes, micro-blasts, etc., even nature herself is reflecting back to us our own state.

When I hear of another suicidal youth I want to reach into the vortex within them and reset them into the orbit of Christ's love. I want to pull them out of themselves and throw them quickly into His embrace so that they can become more than formless matter drifting about, so that they can coalesce into the magnificent being they are created to be so that they can know true joy! A lot of strength is required to come up against the momentum of these energies, but we know in the end, faith, hope, and love are forces that can move mountains and will re-create the world, forming it into a Kingdom of love, joy, peace and justice.

There is a struggle for the spirit of man today. He has been knocked out of orbit and now has to decide what His center will be? Sports? Food? Wealth? Prestige? Fame? Sex? Alcohol? Drugs? Gambling? Modernism? Materialism? Ecology? Politics? Science?

Other manifestations of self?

The drama of our age is to see whether man will realign himself. Will he return to his true center and come back to an ordered rotation around the true Sun, the Son of God Who is Light, Love, and the pure Joy that is Life-giving? Or, will he continue to spin off blindly into massive self-destruction? It is a choice we all must make.

Questions for Reflection

1. If the struggle today is for the spirit of man, what spirit do you see predominating in the culture we live in?

2. How do we reach to the desperation in the lives of so many today?

3. High school counseling offices are full of troubled students today. What, in particular, helps produce the spirit of depression and anxiety so that our young people no longer have the joy of their youth? What would be an inspired response?

4. Would you describe your relationship with God as one of friendship?

Blessed Pier Giorgio Frassati, divine mountaineer,
rescue us from plunging to our deaths in the depths of our self-abysses.

COMING OUT OF HIDING

Making New Year's resolutions can be a tricky business. We may think our best interests will be served by addressing our diet and exercising more regularly. Our family and friends might prefer that our resolve center instead around curbing our negativity, our moodiness, our critical spirit, or our rash judgments. We might decide we need to give extra time to charitable projects when our family or community would be happy to see us enjoy more time in their company. We may even realize we need more prayer in our lives and determine to make space for it when God would prefer we look for Him outside the concept of an exercise to perform.

There is actually one answer to all the needs for change we contemplate at the beginning of a new year: Jesus Christ and the Trinitarian life He came to bring us. Many of us know about Jesus. Fewer of us really feel comfortable saying we know Him. And out of those of us who know Him, we don't always relate to Him or allow Him to relate to us in any way that really affects our lives. There is a kind of split in us between our faith and the rest of our lives.

Vatican Council II sought particularly to address this difficulty of believers today, the problem of a duplicity that manifests itself in those of us who intellectually assent to the existence of God yet fail to live as though we really believe He exists. Instead, we live, practically speaking, as atheists. We do not live as though God is our Father, providing for us in all that is most necessary. If we did, we would not be filled with anxieties and stress over how to take care of ourselves.

We also profess a belief in Jesus as our Savior, and yet we are continually trying to save ourselves. Witness the incredible number of self-help books and social programs that promise fulfillment and ultimate happiness. The promotional tag line is often the only successful part of the whole offering, which inevitably engenders its own problems. In the meantime, participation in the life-giving, healing sacraments wanes, and attendance at Mass is no longer seen as essential.

We say we believe the Holy Spirit is our Advocate and Guide. And yet we fight our own battles without seeking His help while the course we try to steer in our lives isn't on His map. It's of our own making and doesn't lead us to happy or peaceful outcomes.

All of this comes because we fail to realize that our Trinitarian God is a personal God. He wants to be up "close and personal" with us. And He wants us to be personal with Him. The Father is a Person who wants us to relate to Him that way. Jesus is a Person, and He wants us to relate to Him that way. The Holy Spirit is a Person, Who also wants us to relate to Him that way.

It is worth noting that no two relationships with God are alike. Just as a group of siblings who have the same mother and father have unique relationships with them, so too is our relationship with God unique to each of us. Trying to be someone else, even a saint, will drive us away from an authentic communion with God. If He had wanted hundreds of St. Francis of Assisi's or St. Thérèse of Lisieux's, God would have created them. But marvel of marvels, He's created each of us to be our own exceptional expression of His love.

This means, to find ourselves, we have to stop hiding from God, and in a way, from ourselves too. We often hide from Him without even being aware of it. Sometimes we hide out in our illusions. Sometimes we hide behind our wounds, our excuses, our busyness, our technology, science, our pride, or distrust of

God. We hide behind our self-sufficiency until God either takes it away or shows us the limits of our own power. Sometimes we hide behind our sins either out of shame or because we don't want to give them up.

Hiding from the Lord is as old as Adam and Eve. We become afraid of what He might say to us, what He might ask of us. We become infected with doubts about Him. And so we hide. But as soon as we hide, He comes looking for us. We are like children in the game of Hide and Seek. The adult always knows where the child is. But the child still needs to be found. And in the spiritual life, even though we choose many things to hide behind, deep down, we all want to be found. We all want to know we are beloved and sought after because this tells us something essential about ourselves. And this is precisely what God wants for us. He wants us to come out of hiding so He can not only reveal Himself to us, but so that He can reveal us to ourselves as well. It is only in friendship with Him, in a living relationship with Jesus Christ, as confident children of Our Father, and in trusting openness to the Holy Spirit that this happens. These are exciting revelations because infinite Love is behind all of them.

Perhaps we can glean help for the New Year from some of the recent writings and homilies of Pope Francis. But we will have to come out of hiding. The whole of us. No holding anything back, because every area of our life must be touched by God's transforming presence. A good resolution then would be one that seeks to "encounter the Lord and, most of all, allow us to be encountered by Him." Then we must keep our eyes open for the many different ways He encounters us, finds us, in our life experiences, in our prayer, in creation, in the words of another spoken to us, in the Scriptures and Sacraments and Mass and in thoughts that come to us within, from the light of our Baptism.

As Pope Francis so beautifully says: "God does not hide Himself from those who seek Him with a sincere heart even though they do so tentatively, in a vague and haphazard manner." Why? Because "His delight is to be among the sons of men" as the Christmas season has just gloriously proven to us once again.

Questions for Reflection

1. Have you ever seen someone figuratively come out of hiding and begin to reveal themselves? What was your experience of that?

2. Do you know anyone who is genuinely transparent? What would it take to become this way, knowing we will all be completely transparent to one another in heaven?

3. What is your experience with secrets?

4. Have you ever seen or experienced the effects of holding bad secrets?

5. What do you think God wants from us in our secrets? Remember that nothing is hidden from Him?

Saints Francisco and Jacinta, you and Lucia fearlessly kept the secrets you were told to guard and you told the secrets you were given to tell. Help us to share your obedient discretion.

THE SACRED HEART OF JESUS AND THE URGENCY OF DIVINE LOVE

In 1673, Jesus began appearing to St. Margaret Mary Alacoque, a humble nun of the Visitation Order, in Paray Le Monial, France. He revealed to her the tender wonders of His love for her, desiring through her to share these same wonders with the whole world.

In the course of His revelations to St. Margaret Mary, Jesus complained of our ingratitude. But His complaint was weighted with the sorrow of a lover who knows not what else He can do to gain the attention of his beloved, a beloved who is chronically distracted and uncomprehending. In the great apparition which occurred sometime during the octave of the Feast of Corpus Christi, 1675, He said, in what must have been an imploring spirit, "Behold the Heart which has so loved men that it has spared nothing, even to exhausting and consuming itself, in order to testify its love."

We should ask ourselves: What is it we behold, what is it we see when we look at the Heart of Christ? What is Jesus trying so hard to show us?

It is interesting that Jesus says: "Behold the Heart," and not: "Behold My Heart." Jesus, in His Incarnation, comes to reveal the Father to us. Scripture says Jesus "is the image of the invisible God." (Col 1:15) He tells the Apostles: "If you see Me, you see the Father." (Jn 14:9)

So is He not saying: "Behold the Heart...which is the Heart of the Father. If you only knew the depths of His love"?

One of the most compelling revelations of the Heart of God in Scripture is found in the father of the prodigal son. The younger son, returning home after losing everything, though genuinely repentant, is in survival mode. He approaches the father wholly broken by his own sinful choices. He has utterly spurned his father's love and squandered every gift that has been given to him.

Yet the love in the heart of the father who has been anxiously watching and praying for his son's return sees only that his son is back. And though the son has no real expectations, other than to be treated as a slave, the father's response instead is an explosion of love! He orders the best robe, a ring for his finger, sandals for his feet, and the commencement of a feast! His heart has no other response. Not anger, not judgment, not punishment. Only rejoicing, tearful embraces, and celebration! Perhaps we are sometimes held back from approaching or returning to our Father because we have the same poor expectations as the prodigal son did. Our defective appreciation of God's love only harms us!

The sufferings of our lives, especially those that come from our sinful choices, wound our hearts and often plunge us into our own little hells on earth. But the Wound in the Heart of Christ, which we caused, is different. It is a gateway into the Father's love. Entering that Wound takes us on our first steps into Heaven.

Witness the promises of Jesus to those who recognize His love, the Father's love, and seek to live in the Heart that is the source of that love. These promises were given to St. Margaret Mary as part of the revelations of Divine Love and are made to those who are devoted to Jesus' Sacred Heart:

1. I will give them all the graces necessary for their state of life.

2. I will establish peace in their families.

3. I will console them in all their troubles.

4. They shall find in My Heart an assured refuge during life and especially at the hour of their death.

5. I will pour abundant blessings on all their undertakings.

6. Sinners shall find in My Heart the source of an infinite ocean of mercy.

7. Tepid souls shall become fervent.

8. Fervent souls shall speedily rise to great perfection.

9. I will bless the homes where an image of My Heart shall be exposed and honored.

10. I will give to priests the power of touching the most hardened hearts.

11. Those who propagate this devotion shall have their names written in My Heart, never to be effaced.

12. The all-powerful love of My Heart will grant to all those who shall receive Communion on the First Friday of nine consecutive months the grace of final repentance; they shall not die under my displeasure, nor without receiving their Sacraments; My heart shall be their assured refuge at that last hour.

Does that not already sound like Heaven begun on earth? Isn't that what we're seeking?

But there's even more. Poor as we really are, and we are all poor in the presence of God, just as stripped as the prodigal son, we have the possibility of being able to bring joy and consolation to the Heart of Jesus, to the Heart of the Father, by returning to Him, by remembering Him in the ways He asks above. This helps repair, in some mysterious and superabundant way, the hurt Jesus feels, the hurt the Father feels, over the indifference and ingratitude of the vast majority of men. When we behold the Heart that has loved us so, these are small requests. But fulfilling them can transform our lives. And at the end of our lives, these practices will safely lead us through the Wound of Divine Love into the glory of Eternity.

Questions for Reflection

1. Have you ever talked to Jesus about what is in His Heart? We so often tell Him our plans or entrust Him with all our desires, but we don't dialogue with Him about His own sentiments and desires. If you are a lover of Jesus, then you know His Heart. Lovers know the heart of their beloved.

2. If Jesus were to pour out His Heart to you about your own life, what do you think He would say? Remember He loves you to the point of having died for you while you were yet in sin.

3. How can you, should you, respond to this immeasurable love of the Lord for us?

4. How can we fight against our own forgetfulness and ingratitude?

St. Margaret Mary Alacoque and St. Claude de la Colombiére, escort us into the Heart of Christ.

OUR LADY OF SORROWS AND THE PROPHECY OF SIMEON

 very person's life is marked by both sorrows and joys. The two often intertwine in such a way as to make one impossible without the other.

When considering a Feast like Our Lady of Sorrows, it is good to keep in mind that sorrow is always related to love. We do not grieve what we do not love. The greater the love, the deeper the sorrow when the good we love is lost, threatened, abused, or violated in some way.

Who can measure the sorrows of Our Lady? The fullness of grace abiding in her infused her with a love that completely transcended our human limitations. Because of this, her sorrow likewise knew no bounds. The two realities in her have been linked at various times to other titles, most notably "Our Lady of Compassion" and "Our Lady of Hope," both beautiful because they speak to this union of love and sorrow.

Simeon's prophecy, as Mary and Joseph present the infant Jesus in the Temple, is the first public pronouncement to Mary of where her relationship with the God-Man, her child, will take her. Simeon utters mysterious words: "Behold this child is set for the fall and the rise of many in Israel, and for a sign which shall be contradicted; And thy own soul a sword shall pierce that out of many hearts thoughts may be revealed." (Luke 2: 34-35)

These words are intriguing. But they can be understood from the perspective of Mary's unique motherhood. What mother does not know her child so well that even those things that seem otherwise hidden, are not hidden to her?

As children we were amazed by this in our own mothers. We would exclaim: "How did she know that? Does she have eyes in the back of her head?" Actually no. But mothers have eyes at the center of their hearts. Love gives one a vision into things that are otherwise concealed. And that love encourages us, like no other, to remedy any evil or disorder in our hearts. With great solicitude a mother knows us as we really are so that we can become all we're meant to be.

There is some interesting scientific research that gives support to this even on a biological level. At a congress entitled: "At the Dawn of Human Life," organized by the Institute of Gynecology and Obstetrics of the Catholic University of Rome, during the Jubilee year 2000, Professor Salvatore Mancuso, head of the Gynecology Institute, presented some fascinating findings. The research gave proof that beginning in the fifth week of gestation,

> ...when a woman realizes she is pregnant, an infinite number of messages pass from the embryo to the mother, through chemical substances like hormones, neurotransmitters, etc....and the embryo sends stem cells that colonize the maternal medulla and adhere to it. Lymphocytes are born from here and remain with the woman for the rest of her life.

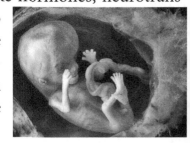

Mancuso stated:

> From the fifth week there is clearly a passing of cells, but messages begin at conception. Even during the first phases of cellular subdivision, when the embryo is moving in the

fallopian tubes, there are transmissions through contact with the tissues touched by the moving embryo. Later, after implantation in the uterus, the dialogue is more intense through the blood and cells, and chemical substances that enter the mother's bloodstream. Finally the child's stem cells pass to the mother in great quantity both at the moment of birth, whether spontaneous or caesarean, as well as at the time of abortion whether spontaneous or voluntary.

When asked how long the fetus' influence on the mother lasts, the professor answered:

Stem cells have been found in the mother even 30 years after the birth. It could be said, therefore that the pregnancy does not last the 40 canonical weeks, but the woman's entire life….It is somewhat as though the thoughts of the child pass to the mother, even many years after his birth.

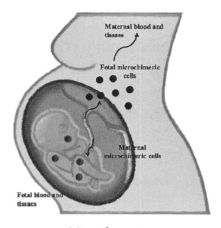

Microchemerism

This is what Simeon's prophecy is about, though in a spiritual sense. It is a prophecy of the universal motherhood that will be given to Mary in the agony of Calvary. As a mother knows every-

thing about her children, and suffers not only for, but with her children, Mary, in an extraordinary way, was so one with Jesus in His sufferings and death that she is rightly called Co-Redemptrix. As her soul was mystically being pierced on Calvary, Jesus opened up a place large enough within her, to take on a universal motherhood for all of us.

In one way, Mary's sorrows flowed from the sufferings of her innocent Divine Son. In another, they flowed from her maternal union with us and our indifference and ingratitude toward God's unfathomable love for us. Her distress over those children who reject their Father's love keeps her always at work and in intercession for the restoration of this relationship. She is near us always, helping us in all adversity, affliction, heartache and difficulty.

St. Pope John Paul II puts it beautifully this way:

> Mary Most Holy goes on being the loving consoler of those touched by the many physical and moral sorrows which afflict and torment humanity. She knows our sorrows and pains because she too suffered, from Bethlehem to Calvary...Mary is our Spiritual Mother, and the mother always understands her children and consoles them in their troubles. Then, she has that specific mission to love us, received from Jesus on the Cross, to love us only and always, so as to save us! Mary consoles us above all by pointing out the Crucified One and Paradise to us! (1980)

Mary continues to mother us, laboring to bring us to true holiness, so that we can be born into eternal life and everlasting happiness. When we are all safely home, it is then, as the best of Mothers, that her joy will be complete.

Questions for Reflection

1. What are the greatest obstacles to hope today?

2. In the sufferings of her life, Mary always linked everything to Christ and to eternal life. Suffering would have been unbearable otherwise. But she saw beyond the present moment to the weight of eternal glory that awaits those faithful in suffering. What is your perspective in the midst of suffering?

3. How did you experience motherhood in your life? How has it affected your understanding of yourself and your own development?

4. Where do you actually need the maternal care of Mary in your life?

Saint Monica, teach mothers how to raise saints.

DENIAL AND THE ROOTS OF VIOLENCE

One of the most distressing realities in the world today is the prevalence of violence. News stories ranging from reports of local crimes to the atrocities of the drug lords to the tortures and executions among rebels and fanatics and dictatorial regimes in various parts of the world seem more and more extreme and almost unbelievable. The destruction of the unborn, perhaps the worst example of all, no longer even gets attention in the average mind. Where does this unbridled, ever-increasing aggression come from? The Word of God gives us some clues.

Jesus points to the heart, as do St. James, and St. Paul. "...out of the heart come evil thoughts, murder, adultery, fornication, theft, false witness, slander." (cf. Mt 15:18-20; also Mk 7:20-23). "What leads to war, what leads to quarreling among you? Is it not precisely the desires fighting inside your selves?" (Jm 4: 1). "...you once nourished hostility in your hearts because of your evil deeds." (Col 1:21).

Whenever we sin we contract something of the contagion of the evil one. His primary disease is pride-induced rage against God. It spills over into a crazed hatred for everything that has its source in God, human beings in particular, and types him as a liar and "a murderer from the beginning." This kind of spirit can begin to contaminate, little by little, anyone of us.

How is it we become infected by this contagion? We are already born handicapped by the consequences of the sin of our first parents. Our own personal sin further weakens our spiritual immunities and compromises our spiritual health so that without regular infusions of grace from the Mass, sacraments, God's Word and prayer, opportunistic temptations begin to gain strength until at some particular moment our defenses are breached and we no longer have the strength to repulse the enemy.

Yet, there is a difference in what happens to a person who has never known the Lord, and one who has known The Lord intimately but then falls through continual carelessness or selfishness or the seduction of some idolatry.

It becomes especially frightening when an entire people who have once known the Lord, forsake Him for these reasons. For they become then capable of every evil imaginable, and worse yet, seeing and calling it good. Bishop Fulton Sheen noted that sin is not the greatest evil in the world, but rather the denial of sin is. It is what put Jesus on the Cross. Can there be a greater act of violence than the murder of God Himself, one which was justified by the religious leaders of the time as good for the nation?

In the readings for Thursday of the 16th week in ordinary time, the Prophet Isaiah, whom Jesus quotes, describes this condition:

> Gross is the heart of this people, they will hardly hear with their ears, they have closed their eyes, lest they see with their eyes and hear with their ears and understand with their hearts and be converted and I heal them.

In the medical world the modern mind would understand this as a state of denial. In the spiritual life it's just as deadly as the state of one who denies symptoms of cancer or heart disease. Yet anyone who knows the workings of denial knows that a challenge to it can provoke vehement reaction.

When denial is firmly entrenched, one can no longer speak the truth directly. The person in denial cannot choose to see it or hear it. Persons in denial are unable to receive the truth in any uniltered form. They become insensitive, and even, as Josef Pieper notes, "unable to search for truth because they become satisfied with a fictitious reality which has been created through the abuse of language." So Jesus often does not speak directly to the people. He uses another tactic. He speaks in parables. He intrigues. He touches the desire in man to solve mystery, to know secrets.

He acknowledges at the same time that those (his own disciples) who can know the truth directly are blessed. Sin has not deadened their sensitivities nor made them skeptics, unrepented sin, that is. For there is perhaps no one more sensitive to grace, more grateful, more humbly dependent on God's mercy and receptive to His communications of truth and love than the repentant sinner.

But one steeped in sin, and more importantly, attached to it, becomes insensible to even the most spectacular graces, skeptical of God's miraculous power, which though without limit, never trespasses man's free will. Truth and grace must be chosen. Speaking truth directly without this can be dangerous, just as it was when Jesus spoke clearly in the synagogue and His own townspeople, in response, attempted to throw Him off a cliff. Denial is a tenacious animal. It can be vicious in protecting its territory. This explains the unreasonable anger that a believer can encounter in an unbeliever. It's difficult to hold a genuine conversation when

hostility surfaces quickly, as though truth itself is the trigger for visceral rejection and rebellion. It's pretty much impossible to approach someone with water, even life-giving waters if they've been infected by the spiritual variant of rabies.

This is another reason why Jesus was "not able" to perform many miracles in certain places, because of the lack of faith, of belief. Not because He couldn't but because He wouldn't impose Himself, or force Himself on an unbelieving lot, a people in denial.

This makes the man who prayed: "Lord I believe, help my unbelief," remarkable for his recognition of his own state and remarkable for his humility in asking for the right remedy. May we have his same courage to break free from the fetters of denial in our own lives, for the sake of our own healing, and our healing as a people whom God has chosen to be His own.

Questions for Reflection

1. Why did Jesus teach in parables?

2. Have you ever wanted to talk to someone who can't hear you, someone who is so entrenched in a belief that they will not allow it to be questioned?

3. What are some things that might lessen resistance to the Truth?

4. People have a right to know the truth. But not everyone wants to know the Truth. Why do you think that is?

Bl. Bartolo Longo, you were entrenched in the dark abyss of Satanic worship, when the Light of Christ penetrated your darkness and blazed a bright path to the Eucharistic Source of that redeeming radiance.
Enlighten us likewise
to the Truth you embraced.

MATURE BELIEVERS

O n November 15, 1972, at a General Audience, Pope Paul VI said the following: What are the Church's greatest needs at the present time? Don't be surprised at Our answer and don't write it off as simplistic or even superstitious: one of the Church's greatest needs is to be defended against the evil we call the Devil.

It is worth reading the entire text of this address to understand yet again how the Lord is always teaching us exactly what we need to understand about the world in which we live. Pope Paul VI speaks movingly about the beauty of the Christian vision of the universe, as well as it's dramatic history gifted with the great treasures of Redemption.

Yet, his focus in this address is upon the proper awareness, understanding, and response to the mystery of evil. A question that begs answering is: why does so much evil go unchallenged?

There are well-established evils already present in the world, abortion and pornography, to name a few of the many. But there are also newly developing ones that scandalize us but don't seem to rouse enough of us to action. The barbaric activity of Isis in the Middle East is a current example. There are others.

One of the fastest-growing criminal activities in the world is human trafficking. Somewhere between 27 and 30 million people have already been enslaved by it. This is an evil that is unquestionably intelligent, organized and has the darkest of forces behind it.

There are many people addressing this abomination, including our own SOLT Sisters in Thailand who have a "safe" house for young girls who come to the city to study and who would otherwise be vulnerable to the sex industry there. But are there enough of us who see with a mature eye and play a decisive role in this battle of the Kingdoms?

Recently, one of our Sisters was on a plane from Corpus Christi to Kansas City. There were four young girls on the plane. The head flight attendant asked Sister to help her to find out where these girls were from and where they were going. Sister was able to obtain the requested information, which had marks of human trafficking. It was reported immediately to the Police. There was an emergency landing in Houston where these girls were recovered by the Immigration Officials. A man on the flight who acted as the protector of these girls was arrested at the next stop-over in Dallas. Sister was accompanied by a police escort the rest of the way to Kansas City to ensure her safety.

This depravity is close to home, present among us. Yet, too much evil goes unchallenged.

Christine Caine, a wonderful, spirit-filled, mature believer who is among those standing up to this evil, has found in her work with women, some horrific realities of the way human trafficking operates. She recounted the story of a young woman in Bulgaria who went out with her friend. A drug was put in her coffee. She woke up in a different country (Greece) chained to a bed and forced to take 25 men a day. This went on for three weeks at which point she was able to contact her mother through a cell phone she'd hidden. Her mother got hold of Chris

Caine's organization, A21, and they were able to rescue the girl and get her to a safe house.

Human trafficking in that part of the world follows this pattern: the traffickers work the girls for two years. Then, those who are able, they impregnate. They then sell the babies to infant farms who, in turn sell the children to pedophile rings, illegal adoption rings, and begging rings. Begging rings use children to get money and they often amputate limbs because such children bring in more money. As for the girls, they overdose them with drugs, and when they die, their organs are trafficked, another huge activity of organized crime.

These things are beyond shocking. But this is what happens when evil goes unchallenged. It proliferates at incredible speed. This is what happens when we refuse to become mature believers who stand up to whatever evil presents itself in our lives and the lives of those we love. This is what happens when we wallow in our own self-centered world, allowing ourselves to be endlessly distracted and deceived, and refusing to let Christ detach us, cleanse us, strengthen us, and transform us into warriors for the Kingdom, into valiant men and women meant for such a time as this.

We were not set into this time by the Lord to be comfortable. We're meant to make a difference in the cause of Christ, in halting the spread of darkness and advancing the Kingdom of God in this generation. We have a lot of territory to reclaim. But we take heart that God will equip us for every good work (Tim. 3:17).

Let us do the work we need to do to die to the "old" man

(woman) so that we can authentically take up our positions in the battle, and in Christ, help to free His people from the oppression of the evil one. May the Holy Spirit and Our Blessed Mother lead us as their little army, in all humility and docility to the complete victories of Christ.

Questions for Reflection

1. What is your observation of courage today?

2. What does spiritual maturity really mean? What does it presuppose?

3. How do you read the present generation and the needs of this generation?

4. What concretely can you do to stem the tide of evil in the world today?

Venerable Carla Ronci,
you dedicated your beauty, your vesture and your Vespa
in heroic service of neglected and endangered youth.
Be a model for modern women. Inspire them to be as you were
and do as you did

CHRISTMAS AND THE FULFILLMENT OF HUMAN HISTORY

God does not usually surprise us without first preparing us, sometimes for a long period of time, for what He is about to do. And yet, we are often surprised because we do not recognize His preparations.

All of history, up to the first Christmas, was a preparation for that Holy Night. That Christmas and every celebration of Christmas since was a great revelation of a simple but astounding truth: God's plan, His desire, His dream, is to dwell with us, to make His home among us so that He might be our God and we might be His people.

The whole of Scripture can be read in the light of this desire of God to live with us, to share with us a life of intimacy, familiarity, and communion. We find it from the beginning, when God walked with Adam and Eve in the Garden in the cool of the evening. We find it in Exodus, where God's presence with His people was manifested in a cloud by day and a pillar of fire by night, which the people followed. We find it in the meeting tent when Moses came out with radiant face after speaking with God.

145

This desire of God to be near His people is seen in the Ark of the Covenant, the building of the tabernacle and the temple, and the liturgy of the Jewish people. We find it in the covenants themselves. And then, in an extraordinary way which few people recognized at the time, the whole of the Old Testament culminates in God coming to us in Person, taking on our flesh and coming to live with us as one of us, in Christ Jesus.

> In the midst of our fallen world, in the midst of incredible darkness, in the midst of a world dying from sin...He comes to make a home for Himself. He comes to set up camp among us and establish a place where people can come to be healed, to be saved, and transformed." (Fr. Michael Keating, CMSWR address 2011)

This is really quite extraordinary. Very few people were expecting this. And most of the world missed it. Only a few holy souls, Mary and Joseph, Simeon and Anna, a few simple souls (the shepherds), and those seeking wisdom (the wise men), witnessed this marvelous mystery of God coming into the world in Person to dwell with His people.

In Jesus, this Divine desire for intimacy with us becomes incarnate. He dwells within the womb of Mary for 9 months and then comes into the world as a tiny infant to dwell with us in utter poverty and need. He lives and grows up among us in the ordinary surroundings of daily life. He learns the ways of a trade with His foster father, dwelling in deep communion in a family, the Holy Family with Mary and Joseph.

When He begins His public ministry, He invites and calls the apostles and disciples to live with Him. They do everything with Him, accompanying Him in His work, asking Him questions, being fashioned and formed by His gaze, His teachings, and the words and works and wonders that come forth from Him.

And then, as He's about to enter into His Paschal Mystery, He devises a way to still stay with them. He gives them the Holy Eucharist and ordains them so they will forever be able to bring Him down into the midst of our valley of tears — so mankind will never be without God. As He is ascending into Heaven He reminds the apostles that He is not really leaving. He says: "Go forth and make disciples of all the nations, baptizing them in the Name of the Father, Son, and Holy Spirit… and lo, I am with you till the close of the ages." (Mt28:20)

This is astonishing; this reality that God does not seem able to keep away from us does not want to stay away from us. He longs to be with us! He delights to be among the sons of men!

Fr. Hans Urs von Baltazar describes it this way:

> For you must understand: He desires nearness; He would like to live in you and commingle His breath with your breathing. He would like to be with you until the end of the world. He knocks at all souls. He makes Himself small and inconspicuous so as to be able to partake of all their little transactions and concerns. He approaches quietly so as not to disturb or be recognized; He comes to be present incognito in the full hubbub of the earth's annual fair. He seeks trust, intimacy; he is a beggar for your love. (*Heart of the World*)

When we understand God's desire to live with us, to be one with us, our vision of life is changed. The world is full of His invitations, His attractions, His drawings to intimacy with Himself. We begin to find ourselves stealing away to be alone with Him. We begin to experience in the silence of our own spirits an ever-deeper desire to be with the Lord and to live in His House all the days of their lives.

The first Christmas contains within it the promise found both in the beginning of man's history in the Garden, and at the end of man's history in Revelations 21:1-4:

> Then I saw a new heaven and a new earth, for the first heaven and the first earth had passed away. The sea was no

more, and I saw the Holy City, the New Jerusalem coming down out of heaven from God prepared as a bride adorned for her husband. And I heard a loud voice from the throne saying, "Behold the dwelling of God is with men. He will dwell with them, and they shall be His people, and God Himself will be with them. He will wipe away every tear from their eyes, and death shall be no more. Neither shall there be mourning or crying or pain anymore, for the former things have passed away."

In the midst of all our preparations, may this Christmas find us seeking the tiny Babe, that we may take Him into the humble dwelling of our own hearts where He longs to be. To the glory of God, which the angels sang on that first Holy Night, may it be said of us: "Behold, the dwelling of God is with men." (Inspired by Fr. Michael Keating, CMSWR address 2011)

Questions for Reflection

1. What do you observe of God's immutability or unchangeableness in your own life?

2. Has suffering, trial or difficulty caused you, sometimes without realizing it, to think God has changed in some way in relationship to you or your loved ones?

3. Do you invite or allow God to live with you in your day-to-day life?

4. Do you think God's plan ever changes? Why?

5. How does Christmas and the actual coming of Christ into human history affect the way you think about suffering and trial?

Saint Faustina, your love for Jesus was as changeless as His Love for you. By your example may we never waver, never weary in our faith, our trust, our love in braving the many varying trials that threaten to change us into someone less holy than Jesus wants us to become.

WHO NEEDS HEALING?

 Imagine a post-apocalyptic world that has been decimated by the unleashing of tremendous forces of destruction. Imagine this world inhabited by wounded and traumatized survivors who face innumerable challenges, including the need to protect themselves from evil, mutated creatures actively seeking their annihilation. Visualize the landscape and atmosphere, heavy with unknowns and potential dangers.

The fall of man in the Garden at the beginning of time can be likened somewhat to this. What existed in unimaginable beauty, harmony, and perfection was blown apart and scattered with such force that we are still, many thousands of years later, reeling from the effects. We live in a wasteland by comparison to what was originally given to us. The fall was something like a nuclear reaction, which began as an internal chain of events. It resulted in a massive, life-shattering explosion. The damage did not stop after the initial blast but continued in the form of long-lasting fallout that weakens our inner being, our will and understanding, and affects all of creation. This was the first sin.

We are all born into this fallen world. We compound the difficulties already present, with our own personal sins, further fragmenting our lives. Because of this, everyone and everything needs healing. From the Pope down to the tiniest baby, from the mega galaxies to the most hidden crevices of creation, there is a need for healing. All creation labors under the weight of a brokenness that was not a part of our origins in God. In the beginning, there was no need for healing.

Colossians 1: 16-17, reflecting the Prologue of St. John's Gospel, explains creation as it was made by God:

> For in Christ were created all things in heaven and on earth, the visible and invisible, whether thrones or dominations, or principalities or powers, all things were created through Him and for Him. He is before all things, and in Him, all things hold together.

In Christ, all things hold together. Apart from Christ, all things fall apart. Adam and Eve quickly and tragically discovered this when they decided to do their own thing rather than follow an order which God had established for them to live in. The brokenness found in our world today is nothing more than being separated from the One Who holds all things together in Himself.

There is nothing God wants more than our healing. Pope Emeritus Benedict XVI has said:

> "Healing is an essential dimension of the apostolic mission and Christianity. When understood at a sufficiently deep level, this expresses the entire content of redemption."

> *Jesus of Nazareth*, pg 176

Jesus is the only One Who knows how to put the pieces of our lives back together as they are meant to be. And where He cannot use the broken pieces, He gives us new ones: new hearts, new minds, new lights, new visions, new courage, new hope, new strength, new or renewed relationships, and so much more. Our unhappiness always comes from not being able to live as we were created to live in a communion of life and love with God, others, ourselves and all of creation.

What can be done? The answer is relatively simple. Draw near to Christ. More importantly, let Him draw near to you. He is like a magnet that begins to pull all the fragmented pieces of your life back together into a beautiful recreation and restoration of God's first intentions for you.

Approach Christ in the sacraments, in the Mass, in His Word, in prayer, in adoration, in the love you share with others. Let Him encounter you. Take time out for retreats. Allow Him to pour His healing grace into your life. Trust Him. Don't worry about distractions. Jesus will work. He needs only the smallest invitation. He will come with delight to  attend you and shower your life with blessing. Let Him come in! You will not be sorry! In the end, even creation will rejoice with you.

Questions for Reflection

1. We carry different kinds of brokenness in our lives, brokenness that comes from original sin, our own sin, and the sins of others against us. What has been the most difficult for you to recognize and deal with?

2. How have you experienced Christ making you, and all things, new?

3. Christ is the one who heals us. How do you take your loved ones to Him? Remember the paralytic whose four friends lowered him through the roof so he could have access to Jesus. What unusual things might you need to do?

4. Why are we afraid to draw near to Christ?

Blessed Buonsignore Cacciaguerra,
your life of opulent debauchery was more drastic and grotesque than the most perverse of Roman emperors. Your sudden losses were as dire and shocking as Job's. Your conversion was as stunning as St. Paul's, because it would have seemed more likely that King Herod would become a follower of Jesus than would you. Yet you became the holiest of penitent priests; and like John the Baptist to the Christ, you became the herald of St. Philip Neri, whose Eucharistic ministry you inspired and assisted in the re-conversion of decadent Rome.
Allay our fears of nearness to Jesus.

FACING OUR IMMORTALITY IN THE LIGHT OF CHRISTMAS

Anyone who has ever received an unexpected diagnosis of cancer or some other serious disease knows the power of the experience to suddenly and radically change the inner world in which we normally live. Anyone who has lost a loved one especially without warning experiences the same thing. Perception, understanding, the hierarchy of what we have up to then considered important suffers a seismic shock and shifts the plates of our current existence into a completely changed landscape, which can seem foreign and strange and certainly frightening in many ways.

Having been through this myself several times, and watching those around me, I've come to realize that the shock comes not so much from facing our own mortality as it does from not having faced our immortality. That's the real problem. To say we now are brought to a place where we have to face our own mortality is actually to stand before an untruth and feel forced to embrace it. Our whole being revolts against it and all the classic stages of denial, anger, bargaining, depression, and resignation follow.

155

And with good reason. We are not mortal, and the light of Christmas announces that definitively. Jesus doesn't come into our darkness to commiserate with us. He comes into our world to rescue us from the fetters of our darkness, including the weight of our own corruptible bodies, so that time (however much we have), in its proper place, can launch us safely and happily into eternity.

Death is a kind of limit, the line past which nothing more can be done in this world in our present state. But it is not the end. We are immortal, and it is not necessary to defend this belief because anyone truly in touch with themselves knows deep in their being that something infinite, something eternal abides in their very substance. And this something is personal. It is not an energy or a memory or a force. It is of the essence of who we are, how we know ourselves, and how we are known. It is our very person, and it is never lost by trial or suffering or disease or death. The person does not die. The body gives way for a time. But we do not die.

Because our body is corruptible in this fallen world, we shed it in dying, in order to be completely healed and made ready for immortal bodies which we will receive, at the end of time. And like anyone who goes through the decline of their own bodies in aging, sickness, losing parts here and there, I've come to understand that it is in keeping with God's plans to hold fast to the promise of eternal life and the glorified body rather than trying to hold on to our present existence, attempting by our own might to make our bodies immortal as though we can somehow transfigure them under our own power. Sickness quickly disabuses us of the illusion that we have the capacity to do this. But it doesn't take away from us the desire to be completely restored, whole and transcendent.

The other darknesses we hold onto in our lives are also often rooted in this failure to embrace our immortality. At Christmas Jesus comes to us, "to a people who walk in darkness" to show is a great light. To those of us living in a land of gloom, His light shines." Is 9:1 This is a light that comes from eternity and causes joy and great rejoicing. It doesn't matter if I live in the gloom of a corruptible body, which I am losing piece by piece or in the decay of old age. It doesn't matter if my darkness is the bondage of alcoholism or weariness, doubt, indifference, fear, wounds, worldly aspirations, pride, unforgiveness, bitterness, depression, a hard heart. This is a light that actively seeks out every darkness to dispel it and banish it forever. It is the light of the promise of immortality which we are created for and which Jesus comes to restore to us if we can just let go of our mortal clingings.

I cannot tell you exactly why I am no longer afraid to die. It is not imminent at the moment that I know of. I have, as I said, faced my own death before. The first conscious time was full of all the shock and fear that is normal for anyone who receives an indefinite diagnosis and is told they may die. "If the disease is anywhere else in your body then all bets are off." That is the way it was put to me. All the human emotions and questions coursed through me at that time, leaving me sleepless and isolated within myself, knowing no one else could stand with me in the place I had suddenly found myself.

The most frightening realization had to do with time. Time always seemed without limit. There seemed to be plenty of it, without measure. Now it was quantifiable. There was only so much left. How is it I was not used to thinking of time here as something limited and then gone forever. To manage time now seemed overwhelming. A great number of things which had always seemed possible now had to be definitively rejected. They would not, could not be done any longer. My mother, as she was dying, recognized this watching a slide show of Hawaii. She said matter-of-factly and somewhat sadly: "I guess I will never get to see Hawaii." And we in our denial said: "Well, let's see. Maybe." The fact was she never got to see Hawaii. And she knew it.

My fear in relationship to time had very much to do with its ending for me. I was frightened by my lack of preparedness for what would come next, for what would come as soon as the measurement of things in this world was no longer the reality I lived in. The most unsettling thing was the thought of suddenly standing before God, Face to face, and not knowing what I could say to Him, fearing He would be so utterly disappointed with me for having done nothing, really nothing of any importance for Him. My fantasies of accomplishing great things were suddenly wasted hours of vainglorious daydreaming, all dissipation, nothing of substance to present because I had only been thinking of myself. And nothing of the accomplishments or achievements I held within me amounted to much in this different light of eternity. They didn't have much meaning there, as far as I could tell, not because they were without value, but because I would have done them for myself, and now I, as I knew it, was coming to an end. The prospect of death has a funny way of de-centering you from yourself, causing you to step outside yourself, making you realize at a deeper level than you have ever been aware of before that you are not the nexus for meaning in life. Our egoism runs much deeper than we think.

I did not come to a reorientation in my awareness until, in the peace of an evening sky in which the Father's presence was written large, I, as small as a child, touched by His majestic power, was lifted out of myself, above myself, into another embrace of reality that made my whole life different.......In an instant, there was peace in living or dying. It didn't matter which it would be. I would be held in this love, and nothing, not even death, was frightening in that love. Whatever happened would come from that love, and in that love I was always/already held.

Time was no longer the same issue because I now knew with my very being that,

… when the fullness of time had come, God sent his Son,

158

born of a woman, born under the law, to ransom those under the law, so that we might receive adoption. As proof that we are children, God sent the spirit of his Son into our hearts, crying out, "Abba, Father!" So we are no longer a slave but a child, and if a child then also an heir, through God." Galatians 4:4-7

This is what His love for me, and for you, is really about. This Gift is always being offered. Christmas is always present. Our deepest regret at the end of time will not be what we did or didn't do. It will be how deeply we underestimated and misunderstood the infinite goodness and love and mercy and tenderness of our God. Christmas lights up this incredible love of God. Jesus came, says the Liturgy of the Hours in Evening prayer I of Christmas, to "bring joy to all peoples with the promise of unending life.." In the fullness of time, He came to break the boundaries of time by giving the hope of heavenly birth to each of us. He did not cling to His time here. He was born to die for us that we could live with Him for all eternity. And Mary, most of all, knew this bittersweet mystery from the time She said: *Fiat*!. The old catechism tells us we were created "to know, love and serve God in this world, and to be happy with Him forever in the next." But, it does not tell us what was in God's Heart as He created us. Christmas does. Our older Brother Jesus, the First Born of all creation, comes to rescue us, to bring us back into the Family, our Family, the Father's Family. We were created because God wanted us to be a part of His Family, and that's where we belong. Christmas is that promise of rescue finally made Incarnate, finally come to us in the Flesh that is the Way to our true home. May your

Christmas be filled with the sweetness of God's love made presen in the light of the smile of the tiny Christ Child. And may tha smile be ever-present to you all the days of your life to lead you to your everlasting homeland!

Questions for Reflection

1. What do you observe of the way in which people generally judge the bad things that happen in their lives?

2. Have you experienced good coming from suffering or evil in your life?

3. Do you experience that your Heavenly Father takes care of even your littlest needs?

4. How would you assess your trust in God?

5. "It is suffering, more than anything else, which clears the way for the grace which transforms human souls. Suffering, more than anything else makes present in the history of humanity the powers of the Redemption." — Pope St. John Paul II What do you observe of suffering in the world today?

6. What has been your own personal experience with suffering?

7. Where or how do you find your peace in the midst of sorrow and suffering?

Saintly Claire de Castelbajac, as an art student during the evil upheavals of the 1960's, you stationed yourself like Joan of Arc as a shield of self-sacrifice to defend priests against the attacks of the devil. The blows you were dealt were horrible, but you turned every agony into an act of love, saying, "To make [your suffering] an act of love is to say God was good enough to send me this blow so that I can offer it to Him with all my heart for his glory. Nevertheless, it takes a thick coat of holiness to turn everything into an act of love."

HEALING
THE FAMILY OF GOD

Why does it seem that every human analysis of the current situation in the Church** produces a long list of problems with multiple causes but no apparent overriding remedy? There is a mystery here, which in our habitual human way, we overlook. Could it be that the cause and the solution is right before us?

We know that Jesus is the One Who redeems us, heals us, restores us, and recreates us. And this happens especially at the celebration of the Mass, the highest form of prayer given to us. It happens according to the degree of our receptivity and co-operation with the infinite graces Jesus holds for us from His sacrifice on Calvary, the sacrifice that is re-presented every time Mass is celebrated.

But why is it that we don't seem to see miracles anymore. And why is it that the Church seems to be in serious decline? If Jesus desires so deeply to heal us, what could be blocking Him?

Let's consider one possible cause by looking at our own participation in the Sacred Liturgy.

On any given Sunday, in Catholic Churches across this country and probably throughout the world, hundreds of thousands, probably millions, of people get up to receive Jesus in Holy Communion, participating in what, for many, has become merely a social ritual. Of those who receive, one wonders how many do so worthily. How many are not in a state of grace and how many believe Jesus is really present Body, Blood, Soul, and Divinity, in the sacred species?

For the most part, there is no malice or ill-intention involved. Yet, there are very real and serious consequences that come down upon the whole household of God for every unworthy Communion committed by God's people.

Here's what St. Paul says:

> For I received from the Lord what I also handed on to you, that the Lord Jesus, on the night he was handed over, took bread, and, after He had given thanks, broke it and said, "This is my body that is for you. Do this in remembrance of me." In the same way also the cup, after supper, saying, "This cup is the new covenant in my blood. Do this, as often as you drink it, in remembrance of me." For as often as you eat this bread and drink the cup, you proclaim the death of the Lord until he comes. Therefore, whoever eats the bread or drinks the cup of the Lord unworthily will have to answer for the Body and Blood of the Lord. A person should examine himself, and so eat the bread and drink the cup. For anyone who eats and drinks without discerning the body, eats, and drinks judgment on himself. That is why many among you are ill and infirm, and a considerable number of you are dying. If we discerned ourselves, we would not be under judgment; but since we are judged by [the] Lord, we are being disciplined so that we may not be condemned along with the world. 1 Cor 11: 23-34

Many of you are sick, and some of you are even dying because you eat and drink the Body and Blood of the Lord unworthily?

Does that mean that everyone who is sick or suffering has

made sacrilegious communions? No, of course not. But every Sunday, we enter the House of God to worship as a family, the family of God our Father. And the deeds of one member, whether good or bad, always affect the whole family.

> God has willed to make men holy and save them, not as individuals without any bond or link between them, but rather to make them into a people who might acknowledge him and serve him in holiness. (CCC 781).

We are saved as a people. We prosper and flourish together, or we diminish and decay together. It is all dependent on our collective choices.

The Old Testament shows us Daniel who was a righteous  and holy man before the Lord, even though his own people were not. They continually broke the covenant with God and ended up in exile as a consequence. Daniel ended up in exile with them though he did nothing to deserve it except that he belonged to them as his people.

In the likeness of all the great prophets, Daniel prayed for his people, asked forgiveness and the Lord's mercy, and made reparation to the Lord by his own heroically faithful behavior and witness. This helped to bring the Lord's favor, restoration, protection, and blessing back upon His people.

We also, as the People of God today, have not been faithful to the Blood of the new and everlasting Covenant poured out for us and the forgiveness of our sins. We easily profane the Sacrament every time we unworthily or mindlessly go up to receive Him.

There is a real confusion today about what exactly we are doing when we receive Holy Communion. The confusion is about the meal itself. We think it is for everyone. Jesus ate with sinners.

This is the same. Well, no it isn't. Joseph Cardinal Ratzinger artic ulated the misunderstanding well. (from his *Collected Works*, Vo 11, Ignatius Press pp 273-274:)

> Nowadays [some] New Testament scholars … say that the Eucharist … is the continuation of the meals with sinners that Jesus had held … a notion with far-reaching conse quences. It would mean that the Eucharist is the sinners banquet, where Jesus sits at the table; [that] the Eucharis is the public gesture by which we invite everyone withou exception. The logic of this is expressed in a far-reaching criticism of the Church's Eucharist, since it implies that the Eucharist cannot be conditional on anything, not depend ing on denomination or even on baptism. It is necessarily an open table to which all may come to encounter the uni versal God …

> However, tempting the idea may be, it contradicts what we find in the Bible. Jesus' Last Supper was not one of those meals he held with "publicans and sinners." He made it subject to the basic form of the Passover, which implies that the meal was held in a family setting. Thus he kept it with his new family, with the Twelve; with those whose feet he washed, whom he had prepared by his Word and by this cleansing of absolution (John 13:10) to receive a blood relationship with him, to become one body with him.

> The Eucharist is not itself the sacrament of reconciliation, but it presupposes that sacrament. It is the sacrament of the reconciled, to which the Lord invites all those who have become one with him; who certainly still remain weak sin ners, but yet have given their hand to him and have be come part of his family.

> That is why, from the beginning, the Eucharist has been preceded by a discernment … (I Corinthians 11:27 ff). The Teaching of the Twelve Apostles [the *Didache*] is one of

the oldest writings outside the New Testament, from the beginning of the Second Century, it takes up this apostolic tradition and has the priest, just before distributing the sacrament saying: "Whoever is holy, let him approach, whoever is not, let him do penance" (*Didache* 10).

No one can judge the state of another's soul. We have no real way of knowing whether anyone is in a state of grace. But given the intensity of temptation in the world today, it seems safe to say that it's difficult to stay in a state of grace without living a sacramental life, which includes regular Confession. From that vantage point, it is hard to believe that everyone going up to receive Jesus in Holy Communion is doing so worthily when the lines for Confession are so consistently small. And when we know that Catholics sin in all the same areas as non-Catholics, and at the same rates.

Our stats for abortion, contraception, pornography, addiction, divorce, etc., keep pace with the rest of the world. And in the realm of what we believe as Catholics, we have become just as relativized. Most people certainly no longer consider missing Mass a mortal sin. And many don't even believe Jesus is actually present in the Eucharist, nor that hell is real. The sensitivity to sin is gone, a rotten fruit of the moral relativism that has also penetrated the thinking of ordinary Catholics everywhere. We've become like the rest of the world instead of the sign of contradiction Jesus spoke of. The salt has lost its savor and is not good for much except to be thrown away.

So many, (not maliciously but just mindlessly), receive the Body and Blood, Soul and Divinity of Jesus, without discernment. The Eucharist, the source and summit of our life, the new and everlasting covenant between God and man in Christ's own blood, the sacrifice of supreme worth and upon which our salvation depends, is not received in humble reverence or awe. It is generally not recognized for the intimate communion of persons it affects.

The "trouble" we see in the Church is really about a relationship, a relationship between Jesus and His Bride, or, if you will Jesus and us. If you need help understanding how offensive our insensitivity and unworthiness is in approaching this Sacrament think of it this way. Imagine you have an honorable job that is at the same time one of the "dirty jobs," pig farming for instance You would not work all day in the pens and then come into the presence of your spouse desiring intimacy, without cleaning up first. Your spouse would be repulsed.

This is the way it is with Jesus. Holy Communion is a moment of intimacy with Jesus in which He gives Himself completely and receives us in return. Pope Emeritus Benedict XVI says:

In the Eucharist a communion takes place that corresponds to the union of man and woman in marriage. Just as they become "one flesh", so in Communion we all become "one spirit," one person, with Christ.

This is an incomprehensible expression of God's magnificent, humble love for us, which descends from the heavens, from the heights of Divinity to be one with us whom He so inexplicably loves. We must begin to recognize this with unending gratitude and humble reverence in return. We want to see Jesus offering us an intense and delicately personal gift of Self, made in complete vulnerability and trust.

When we fail to do this, His Heart is stepped upon, and the life of intimacy with Him begins to fade and then fail altogether. And all other realities begin to suffer and disintegrate, to fall apart, to fail to produce the good fruits authentic love always sows and reaps in abundance. Life becomes dull, disappointing, frustrating at every turn, without hope for a future filled with the joy that makes everything exciting and mystically wonderful.

This is not just a matter of failing to keep a few laws, or of a minority of members scandalizing everyone else. It is a matter of our own personal survival and the survival of our local communities and churches. I would suggest that this is what is really going on today. We have become estranged in our relationship with the Lord and are merely going through the motions. But unless we correct this quickly, we too shall perish in the desert like the generation of Israelites of old who failed to keep faith with the God Who had done such wonders in their midst. They never did see the Promised Land. They died in the interior desert of their own making.

Yet, if we address this one thing first, it can lift all of us to deeper holiness and health and clear the way for phenomenal miracles! At every Mass there should be and will be, miracles, miracles of grace, miracles of healing, miracles of renewal and heroic witness. In essence, the new Springtime of Christianity Pope St. John Paul II spoke about will begin to manifest, an explosion of charismatic gifts and conversions, a new Pentecost.

In 1970, there were 175 active Priests in the diocese I live and serve in, 35 of them teaching full-time in high schools. Today there are only 55 serving and within 8 years there will only be 35. Why isn't God answering our prayers? We pray fervently for priestly vocations, and nothing seems to happen. But we must ask: Why would God continue to give us Priests to confect the Eucharist when we turn around, and in massive numbers, make unworthy Communions? In actuality, withholding Priests may be a mercy of God. Were He to give us what we ask without change on our part, we would only bring greater judgment and condemnation down on our own heads.

The United States Conference of Catholic Bishops says that

> For St. Paul, receiving the Body and Blood of the Lord in a

state of mortal sin can be an act of sacrilege and self-condemnation. To sin against the Body and Blood of the Lord in this way is to be liable for the Lord's violent death. The offenders in Corinth incurred this guilt by overeating and drinking and discrimination against the poor. Such carelessness before the Sacrament triggered divine judgments and even death.

What St. Paul indicates in Scripture is that self-examination should always precede reception of the Blessed Sacrament. Therefore, a close connection between Reconciliation and Eucharist is implied. Divine discipline is a loving call to repentance and spiritual growth. The purpose of these consequences is to avert final condemnation with the sinners of the world.

If we address this one reality Mass will become again an occasion of great miracles just as it was in the early Church. And God

ADORATION

ATONEMENT

THANKSGIVING

THE SACRIFICE OF THE MASS IS OFFERED FOR FOUR ENDS

PETITION

will give us many Priests. He will give us many vocations. But this is going to take a joint effort, out of love for Jesus and out of love or the whole People of God, because it is not possible to come o healing and forgiveness, growth and flourishing of our faith communities if we are at the same time spurning the Lord, eating and drinking of His Body and Blood unworthily and mindlessly.

So what can we do?

Here are a few suggestions:

1. Eliminate the direct source of harm first. Stop doing the bad thing, in this case, making unworthy Communions. And begin to help other people to know how to receive Jesus worthily. This includes beginning with family members. It is not always easy, but if we love our families, they have the first right to be told the truth and to benefit from the extraordinary graces present in the sacrament.

2. Ask our Bishops and Priests and Deacons, and in fact, all those with responsibility to instruct the People of God, for teachings, homilies, catechesis, etc., on receiving the sacrament worthily. Much of this is ignorance. But the effects come nonetheless. Scripture never says ignorance suspends the laws of cause and effect. In fact, there are warnings: "My people perish for lack of knowledge." Hosea 4:6

3. Regular confession (once a month). This sensitizes the conscience and makes us far less likely to approach the Lord and His tremendous love for us indifferently.

4. Pray and make acts of reparation for the ways in which Jesus has been offended in this sacrament. This is an act of charity for our brothers and sisters and a special form of intercession for them which consoles Jesus for the many ways in which He is so

deeply hurt in this Sacrament.

5. Spend time, even 15 minutes a week, in adoration before the Blessed Sacrament. Just as one sits on a beach to absorb the rays of the sun, sit before Jesus and absorb the rays of His grace from His living presence in the Eucharist. The invisible workings of grace will do their part in your life and you will begin to know and understand the Lord in a new and life-giving way.

6. Ask Mary to help prepare us and to receive Jesus within us. This is very pleasing to Jesus and one of the best ways to approach Jesus in this sacrament of His love.

7. Cultivate a sacramental vision of the world. Help others to see the invisible and to embrace the truth. All of creation operates this way. Everything visible reveals deeper spiritual realities. The Eucharist does this in a singular way. Even though we cannot see Him, we know and believe Jesus is there under the appearance of Bread and Wine. This is the truth and it does not change based on personal belief. So the choice is to live in reality or to live in the unreal, life-destroying world of the present culture.

Presenting oneself to receive Holy Communion should be a conscious decision, based on a reasoned judgment regarding one's worthiness to do so, according to the Church's objective criteria, asking such questions as: "Am I in full communion with the Catholic Church? Am I guilty of grave sin? Have I incurred a penalty (e.g., excommunication, interdict) that forbids me to receive Holy Communion? Have I prepared myself by fasting for at least an hour?" The practice of indiscriminately presenting oneself to receive Holy Communion, merely as a consequence of being present at Mass, is an abuse that must be corrected (Ratzinger Memo).

Let us help each other! Let's love our Family back to health and blessing in the Lord's goodness and great patience with us. Let us all one day be able to say wholeheartedly: "As for me and my household, we will serve the Lord." Joshua 24:15

May we live to see the day of a great flourishing of the Church and the transformation of our world into a civilization of life and love. And may we all have played our part in bringing it about.

Question for Reflection

1. What can you do to help implement the seven suggestions above? Take them one by one.

Blessed Frances Xavier Seelos,
you boldly bestowed miracles of healing grace upon the wounded and dying soldiers on both sides during the Civil War and upon victims of the Yellow Fever plague which took your own life. Thank you for continuing to perform now from heaven even more miracles of healing than you administered during your priestly life on earth.

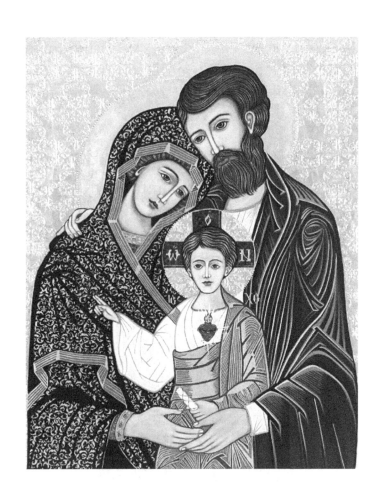

THE COMMAND
TO BE PERFECT

When Jesus tells us to be perfect as Our Heavenly Father is perfect, many of us feel defeated** before we start. We know God doesn't ask us to do the impossible. Nevertheless, we pretty much don't believe it is possible to be perfect.

Yet, it's almost inherent in us to dream about the perfect family, workplace, neighborhood, religious community, parish, etc. And we feel disturbance, tension, even scandal when it's missing in ourselves, friends, spouses, parents, children, the world at large. Our gossip always revolves around a failure in perfection as we see it. Our experience is that we are so often disillusioned we conclude our expectations are not realistic.

But our disbelief in the possibility of perfection is often founded on mistaken ideas of what it means to be perfect and how to attain it. Our notions may vaguely center around dictionary definitions such as: being entirely without fault or defect, flawless. Or we may have worldly ideas that focus on physical beauty, fame, popularity, temporal excellence — all things that are passing away, and so can't be maintained.

Two considerations are important here. *The Catechism of the Catholic Church* helps us to understand the first important point.

> Creation did not spring forth complete from the hands of God. The universe was created in a state of journeying toward an ultimate perfection yet to be attained, to which God has destined it." #304

This is hugely important. It means that we have been created with a need to develop over time! It has pleased God to make us this way.

This movement is evident in our physical development. We begin as a single cell with human DNA that is particular to us personally. Quickly we develop in stages in the womb only to continue that development once we are born. We do not question the movement from infant to toddler to early childhood, middle childhood, adolescence, young adulthood, middle age, etc. One thing is certain. We don't have the same expectations of toddlers as we do of adults. We love them, and we are patient with normal growth.

This same developmental principle holds in our spiritual life as well. We are all at a particular age in  the spiritual life. Some of us are like two-year-olds, busy, curious, interested in many things, but centered in ourselves and prone to discouragement and even tantrums when the Lord doesn't always give us what we want.

Some of us are like middle school children who are primarily occupied with questions of fairness and justice and who tend to put God on trial for what He allows and doesn't allow. Some of us are teenagers full of a mix of ideals and rebellion, generous, sensitive, and even heroic, yet sometimes resisting norms and tried and true wisdom. And finally, some have the wisdom, acquired through suffering and discipline, of the elderly in the spiritual life. Maturity is bought with time and grace, goodwill, and lots of trials, sufferings, and error. We learn as we go. This is part of God's lovely design for us.

The other very important thing to consider when regarding perfection is what Jesus actually said: "Be perfect as your Heavenly Father is perfect."

Our concepts of perfection often have nothing to do with the Father. They tend to be mathematical formulas that give us the illusion that perfection can be attained by our efforts alone. Jesus has already told us that without Him we can do nothing. It becomes evident when we examine the fruits of solo efforts at perfection. The self-made man quickly ends up with unhealthy struggles: hypocrisy, scrupulosity, pathological perfectionism, self-righteousness, rash judgments, disillusionment, even fatalism.

Perfection depends upon one thing: knowing the Father, loving Him, and becoming like Him, like Jesus, according to His design for us. It is a call to relationship, to loving our *Abba*, Father. (This is a specialty of the Holy Spirit: to form our hearts to cry out for Him.)

St. Thérèse knew this in a profound way. She reminds us we do not have to be perfect to approach the Father. We do not have to climb the steep mountain of perfection first to have access to the Father's love.

> The Christian does not think God will love us because we are good, but that God will make us good because He loves us." C.S. Lewis

St. Thérèse imaged Jesus' arms as an elevator that would lift her just as a small child depends on her father to carry her when the journey is too steep or too far. Perfection works in us; in the measure, we draw near and come to know and trust the Father. It is the Father's love that makes us perfect, that makes us who we are meant to be. We are, as Pope St JPII has said:

> ...not the sum of our weaknesses and failures; we are the sum of the Father's love for us.

Like the rich young man, each of us has different things that will be asked of us if we want to be like God in Whose Image and Likeness we are made. This will always involve change.

> To live is to change, and to be perfect is to have changed often. St. John Henry Cardinal Newman

To the question, Can we be perfect? Yes! But it is something that, beginning here in time, will only be fully completed in eternity where we are made immortal and incorruptible and irrevocably united with God forever. The important thing is to begin. Draw close to the Father, let your heart be lifted to Him, and the current of His love will carry you the rest of the way.

Questions for Reflection

1. What does the Perfection of the Father look like to you? " But I tell you, love your enemies and pray for those who persecute you, 45 that you may be children of your Father in heaven. He causes his sun to rise on the evil and the good, and sends rain on the righteous and the unrighteous." Matthew 5: 44-45

2. What kinds of imperfections bother you most, in yourself, in others? 3. Where in your life do you want to be more Christ-like? "Dear friends, now we are children of God, and what we will be has not yet been made known. But we know that when Christ appears, we shall be like him, for we shall see him as he is." 1 Jn 3:2

4. Perfection runs a definite course in each of us. In what areas of your life do you need to be more patient? In what areas do you need to take more initiative?

5. When the rich young man encounters Jesus and asks Him what he must do to be perfect, Jesus tells him one thing is lacking. If you asked Jesus the same question, what might He say to you? Remember that perfection has to do with becoming fully who you are created to be.

Father of infinite goodness, who through the merits of your Son and the gift of the Spirit have set alight with love Blessed Chiara Badano, transform deeply our soul so that, following her example, we too become capable of always doing Your holy will with serene trust.

In the heart of every fallen man there dwells a homing toad.

HOMING TOADS AND THE BEATIFIC INSTINCT

Nothing leaves us more empty of words than deep grief. The heart is swept into a world beyond words, where currents of pain, unlike any other, emanate from the rupture of something deep within. Love is strong as death. One cannot know what that means until death intrudes, threatens, or claims someone you love as you love yourself. The spirit can become so disoriented in shock and grief that it tries to follow that loved one, almost quitting this world while still living in it.

Perhaps the most difficult and painful deaths for us are untimely deaths, the deaths of those who die too young, who don't live out the fullness of their days. A story is told of St. Teresa of Avila in which a couple brought her their deathly-ill baby and asked her to pray for healing. She took the baby in her arms, veiled herself, and the baby while she prayed then told the parents that she asked God to heal the baby if he would grow up to love and serve Him well. But she also prayed that if he would grow up only to lose his soul in the end, to take him now.

The saints tell us that God works mysteriously in His Divine Providence to take us at the time that is best for our salvation without violating our free will. He takes many things into account, including prayers and Masses that will be offered for the person. He works at the same time, graces of salvation and sanctification for other family members and friends through these deaths.

These kinds of deaths can bear great fruit in the matter of

181

salvation, which is not always apparent, es pecially to those caught up in the intensit of grieving and shock. Sr Briege McKenna speaker, and author of *Miracles Do Happe* said that when God withholds the miracl we pray for, it is always because there is bigger plan in play.

One sure effect of untimely deaths i that they wake up the internal GPS of th survivors in unusual ways. And this is good thing. An excellent thing, because w are born with a homing instinct that moves us forward, even i death. Sometimes especially in death. It redirects us and makes u get serious about things that truly matter.

St. Catherine of Genoa speaks about it in this way:

> God created the soul pure, simple and clean of all stain of sin, with a certain beatific instinct towards Himself."

Original sin and personal sin, draw the soul away from God, obscuring this sense. But the beatific instinct is always at work in us, becoming stronger in the measure we turn from sin and turn our gaze back to God again. For those who have gone into eternity and find them selves in Purgatory, the intense and loving gaze of God has suc uniting power, and draws the soul so forcefully, that if

> the soul could find a worse Purgatory in which to rid itsel sooner of all the hindrance in its way, it would swiftly flin; itself therein, driven by the conforming love between itsel and God.

This unfathomable, all-consuming love of God is what move

he needle on our compass. It is what the beatific instinct is set to. And our loved ones, in going ahead of us, are like the magnetic pull that realigns us again with the North Star.

Caryll Houselander, a prolific author and mystic, saw, from his side of eternity, the beatific instinct in another light:

> In the heart of every fallen man there dwells a homing toad. Toads are not very popular animals...on the whole, men think of them as repulsively ugly, squat, square, coarse, and altogether, in spite of the fact that they have beautiful eyes, unattractive.
> The toad (the most common garden variety kind) has an undefeatable drive in him to go back to his home; he can be taken as far away from it as anyone is cruel enough to take him, and he always gets back.

She goes on to say:

> Man, however evil he becomes, however twisted and grotesque-however far away guilt takes him from God, from his home..." always struggles to get back. "He really wants to be in the light of God, in his proper home.

This is something the souls in eternity understand now with such clarity that the many things they can do for us from there, and they are far greater than anything they could have done for us from here), are geared to recalibrating our internal GPS, sharpening our homing instinct, or, our beatific instinct and getting us safely home to God.

Don't ever think your loved ones who have gone on ahead are not beside themselves to get you safely home to where they are in God. Though you don't see them, and you miss them beyond words, they are more present to you than you realize, and are solicitous for everything that will route you safely to the eternal happiness they experience, even in purgatory.

Don't stop praying for your loved ones who may need you prayers and sacrifices to finish the purification of love in Purga tory that will unite them forever with God. And don't stop ask ing them to intercede for you in all your needs. They are gratefu beyond measure for all you offer up to speed their full entry into heaven.

If your own GPS is turned off, turn it back on! Get your signa back. Your own loved ones would speak the words of St. John o the Cross to you:

> Oh souls created for these grandeurs and called to them What are you doing? How are you spending your time?

Questions for Reflection

1. Have you experienced the pull of eternity, the call to something beyond us, in your life?

2. How have you gone through grief? Did it awaken anything new in you? How did you deal with the suffering of it?

3. Why do you think God asks us to move in faith in these areas of the death of our loved ones?

4. If your loved ones who have gone on ahead, could speak directly to you, what do you think they might say?

5. It is good to think about eternity frequently and to try to understand as best we can, the real experience of those who go on ahead of us. How do you currently think of eternity? How can you deepen your understanding of eternity and what it will be like?

Saint Edith Stein, Teresa Blessed by the Cross, you entered every moment as an open door to eternity. In the last moments of your life the door became an altar of holocaust on which you were immolated as a burnt offering for the salvation of the Jewish people.
Keep us mindful of the eternal import of every moment.

THE SEASON OF THE SECRET

The Word of God compenetrates our personal lives and our communal history in beautiful ways, particularly at Advent. Oftentimes we have the experience of finding ourselves, our lives, in the Word of God. This is not accidental. It is essential to our existence and to God's plan. It is one of the ways He gifts us in finding our way through life.

There are many secret mysteries at work in Advent which can be revealed to us according to our silence and interior focus. One of the details of the Christmas story which is often overlooked is the detail of the census at the time of the birth of Christ.

In those days a decree went out from Caesar Augustus that the whole world should be enrolled. Lk. 2:1.

Some translations use the word "taxed" in place of enrolled. Both are significant for us.

St. Gregory says that

the registering of the whole world when our Lord was about to be born was mystical; for He appeared in the flesh Who should write down the names of His own elect in eternity.

And St. Ambrose said: "

There is described a secular registration, implied a spiritual one, to be laid before the King not of earth but of Heaven; a registering of faith: a census of souls...This was then the first public enrollment of souls to the Lord... But in order

that men might know that the taxing was just, there came
up to it Joseph and Mary, the just man and the virgin. He
who kept the word and she who obeyed it.

As one of many dioceses we have felt this same calling to a
census, to accountability, to the registering of ourselves and even
our properties. We have experienced this to be a distressing trial.
We have been "taxed", uprooted, required to leave our discerned
way of doing things at a time when we supposed things would
always remain the same.

We have been asked to "travel" back to our birthright as children of God to be counted. We experience this as strange, un-
comfortable, and unfamiliar. We find it hard to understand. In
the movement and mix of emotion, some have felt deep anxiety,
some have felt dispossessed of their church-homes, and looked
upon with mistrust by others trying to cling to an order which is
being upended. We are required to move, and to be "counted," yet
we sometimes experience that there seems to be no real welcome
in the Inn.

When we look, with great silence in our hearts, we see that
this time for us is deeply mystical. Our present experience profoundly participates in the experiences of the Holy Family. We
see God's providential will working through authority given and
blessed by Him. We see the anxiety of St. Joseph in our Bishop as
he works to secure a stable place for the faithful within the shelter
of a Church in flux and in crisis. We see people in movement,
either complying with the given directions or leaving altogether.
And we see Mary and Joseph, and their quiet and prompt obedience to the will of God suddenly made manifest in current events.

We remember that God did not overlook the fact that Mary
was on the verge of giving birth. The events surrounding this
Birth were arranged to the last detail and meant to be the context
in which the mystery of our salvation would enter into our lives
in Person. But they did not appear this way on the surface. This

most special moment in all of human history was preceded by a sudden uprooting and a hard, treacherous, and exhausting journey.

Difficulties did not disappear with the Birth. New challenges and threats emerged to oppose, to drown out, to kill the mystery, the Gift, the Flood of Light that had just come into the world to enlighten every man.

We are caught up in these same mysteries. Compliance with the "census" is important as a mark of our obedience and trust. But it is not the main drama and should not demand undue attention from us. We do not want to be counted among the faithless.

But when the Son of Man comes, will he find faith on earth?" LK 18: 8.

Rather, we want to be mindful that all of God's ways are full of mystery. The deepest troubles most often hide and give birth to the greatest blessings.

Advent is the season of the secret, the secret of the growth of Christ, of divine love growing within... The way to begin healing the wounds of the world (and of the Church) is to treasure the Infant Christ in us; to be not the castle but the cradle of Christ; and, in rocking that cradle to the rhythm of love, to swing the whole world back into the beat of the Music of Eternal Life. Caryll Houselander

Mary was absorbed in the Mystery of God's love growing within Her despite the seeming chaos around her. That is our same call during Advent.

May our faith in God's omnipotent care never fail us as we await the sweet arrival of our longed-for Love Who comes to us in all the wrappings of our own littleness this Christmas.

Questions for Reflection

1. If a heavenly census took place right now, how would you be counted?

2. What is your interior life like? What absorbs most of your attention?

3. How do the things you spend your time on, look in the light of eternity? Do they matter in that light?

4. Many of us let the things outside of us derail our focus on God. What in particular, makes you lose the presence of God within you?

St. Benedict the Black, as a son of African slaves in 16th century Italy, you were never taught to read or write, yet you never lamented or resented the daunting impediments in your circumstances, but counted them all as incentives to sanctity. You became a renowned cook, then a holy hermit, then a Franciscan monk, then a superior of your community, then a novice master, a revered confessor and a worker of miracles with mystical knowledge of scripture and theology while humbly resuming your role as cook. May our interior life of grace illumine any darkness in our surroundings imposed to hinder our progress in holiness.

KEYS FOR CHANGE

A story is told of a man frantically searching for his lost keys under a streetlamp. When a police officer stops to help the man, he asks him where he last had his keys. "Over there by the bushes," responds the man. "Then why are you looking here?" asks the policeman. "Because the light is better here."

At the beginning of the year, as we contemplate changes to be made, it can be helpful to question our focus. Sometimes change comes not from focusing on something in the environment, but rather on the environment itself and whether it supports the goals and expectations we have.

One of the keys concepts in education is the concept of the prepared environment. In observing children, Maria Montessori noted that when one understood the developmental needs of the

child, they could arrange the environment in such a way that it would not only be conducive to real growth and development, but would accelerate thriving and happy explosions of learning, or sensitive periods as she called them, for optimal growth.

To emphasize the importance of this idea, she used the example of a waterwheel often placed alongside a river to generate energy. She noted that if you were to relocate the water-

wheel to the desert, it would fail to function because it would b
in the wrong environment. So she arranged the classroom ac
cordingly and demonstrated the remarkable fruitfulness of pay
ing attention to the environment if you want to truly serve chil
dren in healthy development.

The idea of prepared environments is a universal concept tha
has been around since the beginning of time. In fact, the under
standing of the importance of environment runs through Scrip
ture as an undergirding theme, from the Garden of Eden to th
Promised Land to the instructions for worship and communit
life, to Jesus' teachings about the Church and eternal life.

It also runs through the saints' teachings on holiness, wher
we discover, once we have committed to the work of sanctifica
tion, that we often have to change our environments and relation
ships to avoid the near occasions of sin, which we encounter s
quickly in life today. If we fail to address environment, it become
almost impossible to conquer the disorder and temptations tha
are long-standing and prevalent in us. (An active alcoholic can
not expect to recover if he takes a job in a bar, or continues t
socialize with people who are always drinking. The environmen

verpowers him in his weakness and does not serve but sabotages is efforts.)

Another area where this concern is also present is in the Church's directions to religious communities and parish communities. Religious communities are structured the way they are for the sake of creating environments that help members live the perfection of charity and give prophetic witness of the life to come. Parish communities are meant to support people's search for God and a deepening relationship with Him while providing at the same time, a place for authentic, communal worship of God as His People.

Family life was also ordained by God from the beginning of time, as the best environment for children to be raised in and for human beings to live in. Jesus points to this importance of environment both in his life, (Bethlehem, Egypt, Nazareth, the Holy Family) and when He tells us to seek first the Kingdom of God. As He returns to the Father He tells his disciples not to be sad, because He goes to prepare an eternal place for us in His Father's Mansion. -Jn 14:3 What anticipation we should feel at that thought!

Why is this particularly important for us today? Because we see the increasing effects of chaos and barbarism, which are the fruit of environments that are disordered and detrimental to the dignity and development of the human person and human communities. Environment isn't the whole answer, but it is remarkable how a good environment can draw the best out of people while the opposite often happens in unhealthy environments.

Vatican Council II talked about the role of the laity in sanctifying the temporal order. Another way to understand that is to say the laity are responsible for creating environments which are conducive to the living out of our relationship with God here and now, and as preparation for eternal life hereafter.

Laity should be sanctifying all areas of human activity: law, politics, medicine, technology, education, science, etc., by supporting and establishing Christian environments that respect the human person and are structured to the recognition of God's order and the full development of the human person, vs. the profit or power at all costs mentality.

The beginning of a new year is an excellent time to examine our environments and ask some tough questions. How much is happiness or a lack of joy and satisfaction tied to disorder in my environment? In the life of my family, friends, etc.? What is my work environment like? What about my social environment? Where can I bring some humanizing and Christianizing influence into the environments I live in, work in and recreate in? What kind of self-discipline is necessary to keep that order once it is established?

It is, of course, necessary to look at the environment of our own hearts. The interior of our own hearts tend to dictate the order or disorder around us. At the same time, some environments are more healing to the heart than others. And our goal should be to create these kinds of environments.

This life, as we have often said, is a preparation for the life we will live in eternity. If there are things in our life here that are not compatible with our dignity as children of God and future citizens of Heaven, then now is the time to clear them out and begin anew to recognize the great gifts and the high call God has given to us already here in time to participate in building the Kingdom of God on earth as it is in Heaven.

Questions for Reflection

1. Do I have set goals for this time in my life?

2. What is my current environment like? Given the things I am dealing with right now, does my environment support the goals I have at this time in my life?

3. What kinds of things in my own heart might need attention?

4. Given that emotions/moods can be contagious, how do I affect the environment of people I live with, socialize with, work and worship with?

Sister Blandina Segale,
you were a missionary pioneer boldly blazing a trail to
expand the boundaries of the Kingdom of Christ across the
inhospitable Western frontiers of North America, turning the deserts into
fertile fields where the seeds of the Gospel might flourish. Give us a share
of the guts and gumption it took for you to go up against the murderous
intent of a gunslinger like Billy the Kid.

"What is Truth?"

Before the first-ever State visit of Pope Benedict XVI to Great Britain in September of 2010, the British media voiced opposition to the visit with increasing hostility, indirectly encouraging petition protests and civil dissent among the people. Pope Benedict had been known as Ratzinger the Rottweiler during his tenure as Head of the Congregation for Faith and Doctrine in the Vatican, because of his firm stand on the traditional teachings of the Church. Rottweilers, of course, summon all sorts of connotations in the minds of ordinary people: stubborn, dominant, aggressive, territorial, bullying, strong, loyal, etc. All together off-putting to say the least.

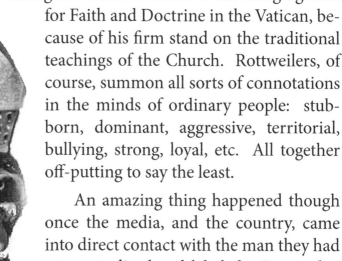

An amazing thing happened though once the media, and the country, came into direct contact with the man they had conceptualized and labeled a Rottweiler. He "turned out to be a shy, warm and frail 83-year-old who perked up every time his security detail allowed him to greet people, especially youngsters and his own generation." Outspoken journalists who had vehemently opposed the visit were completely won over by the Pope and gushed: "Ratzinger the Rottweiler transformed into Benny the bunny," "We all want to cuddle up to him and get him to bless our babies." (AFP News Wires, Sept. 2010) The real man won out over the fabricated image that had triggered such powerful emotions nationwide.

This illustrates an area that is particularly dangerous today. It is the tendency to conflate strong emotion with the truth. If feel strongly about something, it must be true. The trend toward gauging truth by how one feels or has been made to feel about something and not by an objective consideration of facts or evidence produces all sorts of crazy, irrational judgments, and behavior, which once would have been self-evident but today seem lost on those formed under a hierarchy of values that places feelings at the top. Feelings become more important than truth or considerations of right and wrong. Various elements of society are keenly aware of this and intentionally manipulate people by deliberately inciting certain emotions. They understand emotions can be very contagious, and if they can move even a small group toward a certain goal, it will spread incredibly quickly.

A prominent example of this is found in the way emotion was used to change people's views of and opinions regarding abortion. Before its legalization in the US in December of 1971, any doctor who practiced such procedures was ostracized by the mainstream medical community. Abortion was known, at the level of conscience, universally, to be the destruction of a human baby. The affirmation of science (which is there), was not needed. The issue of the humanity of the baby was not in question. Yet, that became lost because of a genius strategy on the part of those working to legalize it.

Dr. Bernard Nathanson, who was one of these key players and who later converted to Catholicism and worked the rest of his life to undo the legalization of abortion which he had fostered, explained it this way. He said they used three main tactics in their work and the third tactic was by far the one that accelerated them to their goal the fastest.

The first tactic was to falsify statistics. So they simply inflated ne numbers for back-alley abortions to make it seem that this as a national crisis that had to be addressed. Second, they set ut to discredit the Catholic Church as patriarchal, sexist and ld-fashioned because they knew that is where their main opposition would come from. But the third, and most masterful trategy, according to Nathanson, was to couch abortion in terms f women's rights. Once you talked about abortion as a woman's ight, you could easily incite indignation if any opposition to a woman's right to choose" was expressed. Rational debate was no onger possible because once the emotions were running high, ninking things through clearly and calmly debating them, failed. eelings ruled out facts. And the immediate stance of those emo-onally swayed to favor abortion became accusatory: You are raging a war on women! You are violating our freedom and our ight to choose what to do with our own bodies, etc. It became ll about "me" and not about the little life entrusted so intimately) the woman.

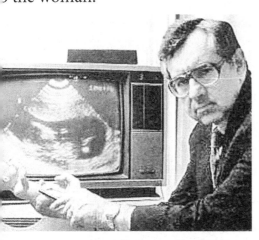

Dr. Nathanson himself was finally converted when he deliberately filmed, via ultrasound, an abortion. The image of the little baby trying to escape from the instruments dismembering him, the shocking encounter with the truth of what he was oing, was enough to make him stop on the spot and to spend he rest of his life trying to make restitution for what he had done.

Emotions are powerful forces that are a deep part of what nakes us human. They can move us in ways that are strong and lecisive, as when we need to take action in the face of injustice r danger, but also in ways that are delicate and sensitive as when ve need to attend to a small child in distress. In the right order, emotions help us to go beyond ourselves in deeds, behavior and relationships for the sake of a greater good. However, in the disorder, they can overpower reason and practical wisdom. They can blind us to the truth and take on a life of their own which manifests in excess and the domination of self-interest or self-absorption over all else.

The crucial point to understand is, discovering truth is not the goal of the emotions. They were not given to us for that purpose. Our intellect and our powers of reason and understanding were given to us for that purpose. Our emotions are meant to be informed by and to serve the truth as forces that move us to the good or away from evil. And until that right order is re-established in each of us, we will continue to see an increase in chaos and the culture of death around us.

200

Questions for Reflection

1. Am I aware of what kinds of things trigger me emotionally?

2. Which emotions are most easily triggered in me? Anger? Sympathy? Love? Compassion? Sadness? Joy? Fear? Disgust? Trust? Anxiety? Etc.

3. Do I sometimes make decisions with my emotions? Do I have a habit of acting impulsively from emotion?

4. In my life experience, what have been some of the effects of making decisions with my emotions? What would I do differently now?

St. Dulce Lopes Pontes, the Mother Teresa of Brazil, inspire us to emulate you by letting God turn our natural human emotions into supernatural instigators of miraculous grace.

THE SPIRITUAL CONTEST AND THE MIND

he first, and undoubtedly the worst, bad decision ever made, was made in a battle between two superior intelligences before historical time began. Though we image the conflict with St. Michael dressed in armor  and wielding a spear over Lucifer, the most beautiful of the angels now turned into a writhing, contorted, dragon-like creature, the battle was not physical but rather intellectual in nature. The arrogant supposition on the part of Lucifer, that he was greater than God in determining the "right order" of things, was resoundingly contested and conquered when St. Michael thunderously proclaimed: "Who is like unto God!" The power of those words suffused with truth and piercing light and rumbling through the far reaches of the heavens was enough to cast the demons from the seraphic realms forever.

Intelligence, a God-given gift which makes us different from the animals, and gives us a likeness to God, can be cradled in either pride or humility. Humility recognizes the gift; pride glories in the gift without acknowledging the origin. Humility generates light; pride is blind to it.

We do well to remember spiritual warfare is not out there

somewhere. It takes place inside of us, in the understanding and the will, the mind, and the heart. Jesus tells us the Kingdom of God is within, and

> From the days of John the Baptist until now, the kingdom of heaven suffers violence, and the violent are taking it by force. Matthew 11:12.

You cannot run from this battle. Every man is put to the test within his very self.

We may feel at a distinct disadvantage in a battle where our foe knows every weakness we have and has a superior intelligence with which to fight against us. And yet, our victory is had beyond the limits of purely human reasoning and strength. When the mind, the intellect is filled with the light of faith, we are able to see things and assent to things we do not fully understand, and thus to be victorious. And when the will is informed by charity, by the love of God, it moves easily to that which is shown to it by faith.

When Jesus contends with the devil in the desert, he does not engage in dialogue, because what the devil says, is technically true. He simply reverts to the love and providence of the Father and manifests His determination to wait on Him, even in suffering, rather than follow any direction coming from a creature who has willfully cut himself off from infinite good.

All temptation follows the pattern of the first sin in the Garden. The devil attacks the understanding: "Did God really say that? That's not true! He knows if you eat this fruit you will be just like Him, and He doesn't want that. So He's keeping it back from you." Once Adam and Eve allow doubt to be sown into their minds, their hearts lose trust in God, and they choose what they should have rejected.

The same thing happens to us in our personal temptations. A thought comes to us, and we toy with it for a while and then start thinking it wouldn't be so bad to do the thing after all. God will understand, etc. Check for the tail of the serpent when you find ourself thinking like this about things you know are expressly wrong. Our pride and our inordinate seeking after pleasure can blind us to truths which God is very clear about.

It is sobering to observe that these internal battles can affect far more than ourselves. Lucifer must have been so persuasive in his argument that he swayed 1/3 of the angelic hosts to follow him. So too, do we see the same principle play out in human history. The last century has produced ideology after ideology (nazism, fascism, socialism, communism, radical feminism, liberalism, conservatism, traditionalism, modernism, and on and on, masses of people following an often diabolically compelling and magnetic leader set on an appealing but fatally flawed idea.)

Jordan Peterson, a popular speaker and engaging thinker says this about ideologies:

Ideologies are substitutes for true knowledge, and ideologues are always dangerous when they come to power, because a simple-minded I-know-it-all approach is no match for the complexity of existence.

Jordan B. Peterson, *12 Rules for Life: An Antidote to Chaos*

This certainly has been evidenced over and over again in the last century, with the resulting human destruction numbering in the hundreds of millions. But this is simply spiritual warfare on a grander scale. Someone takes the bait in a bad idea, which usually has to do with creating a better existence but hides a lust for power. The attempted implementation of the idea ultimately destroys everything in its reach. The followers, and surrounding people pay the price with their lives because they are deceived into believing that utopia, (a perfect existence), here on earth is possible and that people will change and be happy if they just acquiesce to the plan.

It is merely a re-packaging of the original temptation. The

serpent whispers the same lie to the modern age: your life will b
better if you do what I say, not what God says. This is the seed o
corruption that ruins everything from individual lives to whol
nations under the sway of contaminated ideas. Pope Benedic
XVI noted that:

> "Wherever politics (read ideologies) tries to be redemp
> tive, it is promising too much. Where it wishes to do th
> work of God, it becomes not divine, but demonic." *Trut*
> *And Tolerance: Christian Belief And World Religions*

Be aware of your thoughts. They have the power of heaven o
hell in them. St. Mark the Ascetic says,

> Every thought has its weight and measure in God's sight.

If we can sin in our thoughts, we can likewise do good in ou
thoughts, exercising faith and holding onto trust in God. Ma
Our Blessed Mother help us to put on the mind of Christ that w
may fight the good fight and be victorious in the arena of our ow
souls.

Questions for Reflection

1. How aware of your thoughts are you?

2. How do you discipline your thoughts, if at all?

3. What would you say is the general tone of your thoughts throughout a day? Positive, negative, distracted, curious and unruly? How would you describe your thought life?

4. What does "putting on the mind of Christ" mean to you and where do you personally see the most prominent attacks against that in your thinking?

St. John Henry Newman,
following the example of St. Philip Neri, who stressed that humble
willingness to be made holy consists in allowing your intellect to become
more and more conformed by the Spirit to the mind of Christ,
help us, like you, to consign our every thought and word
to the purifying flames in the furnace of the Heart of Jesus.
May your intellectual brilliance become
a beacon of the Light of Christ to beckon into bloom
those buds of baptismal grace whose growth to fruition
has been stunted under the dense shadows of our transgressions.

EASTER
IN A TIME OF PANDEMIC
"No Coward Soul is Mine"

It's hard to overstate the crushing trauma and demoralization, the numbing shock, and the paralyzing fear, the apostles experienced as they watched the sufferings and death of Jesus unfold before them in a quick succession of sudden and violent events. Once the betrayal was set in motion, their entire understanding and expectations were brutally assaulted and swiftly destroyed in a matter of hours. So overwhelming was the Paschal Mystery for the closest friends of Jesus that they could not stay with Him as He went through it. St. John, the beloved disciple managed, not on his own, but by relying on the only one who had any courage and faith left: Our Blessed Mother, who had also gathered a handful of grieving women round her.

As the events played out, darkness descended and stalked the followers of the Nazarene, now dead and locked inside a dark tomb behind a monstrous, immovable stone with Soldiers assigned to keep it sealed. An eerie stillness, a strange, suffocating breathlessness, unlike anything anyone had ever known, blanketed the whole earth and penetrated their own hearts, so there was no escape from it. Hope and faith beat feebly in the spirits and souls of those, (save one Woman), closest to the horrific Death of the Anointed One, the Messiah who was going to save the Chosen People. The whole world groaned, "Foundations once destroyed, what can the just man do?" Ps11

Jesus' followers, who had known oppression, persecution and exile in their history as a people, who had been separated from the temple and the worship of the One True God, were no ready. They were shocked by these events which had been fore told. And they were afraid. Though Jesus had tried to warn an prepare them, they did not understand Him deeply enough to hold onto the center of His entire message. We don't understand either. We, too, have difficulty holding onto the truth about the Cross in our lives.

Despite this, the Resurrection of Jesus takes place. In the midst of trauma, fear, isolation, grave uncertainty, and a feeling of profound abandonment on the part of the disciples/apostles, Jesus rises. He definitively conquers death and wins for us freedom from sin, and the glory of everlasting life.

This Easter will be like that first Easter in many ways: we will be locked behind our doors, afraid, protecting ourselves, stupefied by what has so suddenly happened, mourning the loss of Our Lord Who has been taken away and sealed in tomb whose entrance is barred to us.

This year there will be no public witness to the sufferings an death of Jesus, our Savior and Redeemer. Easter will not be communally celebrated with processions of light, incense, resounding notes of alleluia, flowers and bells ringing in the colors of spring and newness of life. Yet, Jesus, Who rose in an instant in the darkness of the night giving way to the dawn, will walk right through the barricades of fear, of unbelief, and unfaithfulness by first walking through our material protections: tombs, doors, and he roads we take away from the "awful" events of our lives.

He will do this for us this year just as He did on the very first Easter. We will not have the joy of physically celebrating together the most beautiful liturgy of the whole year, nor of receiving Jesus sacramentally. But this will not stop Jesus. There will be nothing to disguise or distract us from His presence if we have the hope of Easter in our eyes, and are truly yearning to see Him as the holy women did on Easter morning.

Jesus will spend the next forty days, strengthening us in our faith, just as He did, starting with Mary Magdalene, who didn't recognize Him because she was not expecting to see Him. Peter, and the rest of the Apostles, assailed by shame and doubts will also need direct evidence before their faith is strengthened. But what joy then engulfs them when their eyes are opened, and they see beyond the limited appearances and understanding of this world.

This crisis can deepen our faith in the same way. Jesus has no barriers and is not held back by anything. He wants fearless warriors who charge right into the face of evil to conquer it in the name of the Risen One Who lives forever, no more to die. This is what the apostles became. This is what we too can become if we trust.

Emily Bronte expresses something of this in her poem: "No Coward Soul Is Mine"

> There is no room for death,
> Nor atom that his might could render void;
> Thou — Thou art Being and Breath,
> And what Thou art may never be destroyed.

Knowing God does not abandon His people ever, in exile, in suffering, in death and dying, we believe Our Risen Lord is always with us and promises us His glory if we persevere. Only one other person has walked through these kinds of times without faltering, and no others have done it without her. We ask Mary to attend us, teach us and keep us safe both in faith and from the invisible enemy looking for entry. We pray this virus die a timely death and forge us into great saints in the meantime in the midst of our hurt, our sorrows, fears and grief,

May we experience this Easter what St. Augustine so beautifully exclaims:

"In my deepest wound I saw your glory and it dazzled me."

Questions for Reflection

1. We are much like the original disciples. Who do you identify with? St. Peter? St. John? St. Thomas? The Holy Women?

2. How has your faith been challenged during this time of pandemic?

3. What is the real message of the Resurrection and how are you going to live it?

4. What is your greatest sorrow at this time? What do you hope for and look forward to?

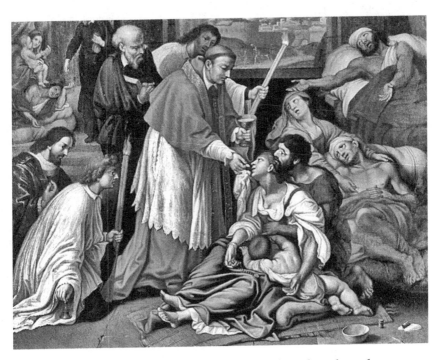

"Be ready to abandon this mortal life rather than the people committed to your care. Go forward among the plague-stricken as to life, as to a reward, even if there is only one soul to be won to Christ."
St. Charles Borromeo

Miscellaneous Poems

He looked upon His own
and His heart was pierced through
by the vacant eyes of the
child starved
for light and battered
by darkness.

Torn, His, a heart that would give
itself as food to be consumed
in order
to restore life
to the hollow face,
in order
to surface the hidden grief
that devours in silence;
in order to heal in love.

Those thoughts and deeds
of death
born of a heart choked
by darkness
have no place
in my dwelling now.
Do not use them
to conjure me up
for I no longer exist
in the chaos of absence and
separation, in the agony
of the void where pain belongs
to the circle

of interior starvation,
where the madness
of fascination with evil
eviscerates its victims
and feeds them to
the jaws of eternal
nightmare.

Rather do I belong to
He Who is fullness of Light
and possesses me in Truth,
Who seals my heart
in praise and hides
me in His Fatherhood
And Who sends me forth
as a tracer
in the night sky.

Wrapped within the scent
of evening, the quiescent
embrace of dusk, peace
lies in the flightless shadow
of the Heart
of my Beloved Who loves concealed
within worded silences, behind
an Armor
to be taken
to the enemy.
In motionless movements,
moments stripped
of time and vision
in the barren desert,
I lay my head
at the ragged feet
of my Beloved (heart caressed,
imprisoned in stillness),
And in the night He sequesters
light edges of enigmatic
touch clothed unbound
in the silence
of infinity.

Heaven

Only

Sings

All

Noble

Need

Athirst

Heart

Of

Sorrow

Anointed

New

Now

Alive

Into cobwebbed haunts
and festering darkness
slips a Lady of Light in search
of her children.

Underneath the curved vault
of the sky (an arrangement
of semaphoric lights), and
in between trains of thought,
dwell the uninterpretable
bonds of silent languages
within which
love comes to be

The day is now wild thin
on edges of unmoving recollection,
teetering on the verge, the
explosion imminent.
In the solace white of the one love
the emptiness is not fooled.
We cannot accomplish anything
forever until we become
fighters of the mourning flesh.

Words hang like bells in the air
Awaiting their time
of descent into the wilderness
Of the hearts of men
Where the unreachable delicacy
is parroted as raw, coarse sound
Stripped of its power to save.
The Word though never dies,
It waits fixed on the bewildered face,
The lost face, the terrified, the yearning,
The angry, the belligerent face,
All the while fashioning in the silence,
And the suffering,
Behind the eyes,
the resonance of the pure heart in which
It takes up its deep, sweet abode.

Veronica's Veil

Elaborate dress and dreams
Pry the desire
to escape self-knowledge
Into the open where hearts
Hardened by illusion and self-pity
Voraciously consume the lie
They are not like other men
Though other men inhabit their shadows
and give them shape.
The mirror of mud and blood
Becomes the Treasure gifted
To those unafraid to cradle
The aching beauty.

Bodies move to the music of higher love,
David before the Ark,
Guilty raiment finding
it's remedy in praise.

Couriers of the Burden

He swims the symmetry of
Saturday nights (sex, sleep),
the ornamental expenditures, visual
lies, carpet pattern mazes, vacant
convictions, the earth of fantasy and the fence
of love against death, aware
of the scribes of light. On
the wall his fascination
remains, ballets of light and shadow, cyclic
rest, smoke light.
In back bar pool rooms he craves
the intensity of the fire and courts clay
children with red ceramic
eyes, (breakable visions): squares of
sun and moon, and female silhouettes.
In halves of time identical, he orders
a round of drinks to maintain
the secure, monotonous rhythm of
diuretic secrets, and ponders the first remote
sentence in a junkyard of contradictions,
unaware of the scrimmaging forces
around him.

Sycamore

Mary, do you remember that
Hot afternoon in the Church all alone when I looked at you
holding Jesus dead
in your arms, and He breathed on me
so that I felt to be suddenly blanketed
in my own death
shocked and unable to breathe at this touch,
the Breath that annihilates, in urgency, necessity
and Divine desire.
Living death, Sweet release I pulled back in fear
as though I could delay this or find another way,
yet longing only for this very intimacy.
Take my fear, Mother!
I desire this kiss on the mouth
in death, and the embrace of Life. Let me look
at His Eyes closed and kiss them in the quiet
of my soul/His soul.
Let me see His Passion more and more;
Let it befriend me and drain my heart.

The Sinner's Song

I am His Beloved
    the Yearning of His Infinite Goodness
    the Gift of His Fatherhood
    the Desire of His Spirit
    the Beat of His Heart.

1 am the Daughter of His Mercy
    the Sweat of His Agony
    the Content of His Silence
    the Mark of His Sufferings
    the Child of His Cross
    the Child of His Light.

I am born of
    the Breath of His Mouth
    the Light of His Eyes
    the Touch of His Hand
    the Desire of His Heart
    the Fire of His Love
    the Movement of His Spirit
    the Thirst of His Sacred Passion
    the Wound in His Side.

I am carried in

>the Love of His Mother
>the Kiss of His Gentleness
>the Balm of His Forgiveness
>the Caress of His Peace.

I am

>the Treasure of His Poverty
>the Soul of His Aspirations
>the Joy of His Life
>the Delight of His Eye
>the Thought of His Heart.

I am found

>in the Words of His Mouth and the Cry of His Voice.

I am

>the Child He rescues, the Child He hides
>the Child He protects, the Child He blesses
>the Child He heals

I am

>the cause of His Search, His Sorrow, His Solicitude.

I am

>His Friend, Spouse, Mother, and Sister.
>He yearns to tell me
>everything He is about.

For me

He is consumed by love.

Heaven itself
cannot keep Him from me for He Leaves
Heaven, comes after me, redeems me
and takes me to Himself.

He makes the whole universe fight on my behalf.

He is with me always
even until the end of time.

He is the constant whisper:
"Turn to Me...I will espouse you to Me forever.

My love shall never leave you, nor my
covenant' of peace be shaken...With great
tenderness, I will take you back..."

It is I for whom

He lays down His Life
that He may feed me
cleanse me, embrace me, clothe me,
and place His ring upon my finger.

And to me,

He gives His Father's Kingdom
that I may learn to welcome Him, love Him,
care for Him, visit Him, comfort Him,
feed Him, give Him drink, clothe Him and
house Him so that I may live, die, and rise
with Him and in Him
unto the glory of God forever.

We become what we contemplate. One who contemplate disfigured things becomes inwardly disfigured. One who contem plates transfigured things becomes inwardly transfigured. On who contemplates the all-beautiful Face of the Incarnate Wor will be supernaturally beautified.

St. Therese of Lisieux

Ite Missa Est

In your beak take,
Small bird,
This pollen spark.
Sing into distances
This prill of keening silence.
Past the disappearance of galaxies
Wing this seed of frail fire.
Sting against the dark immensities
This cinder you have breathed bright,
This infinitesimal chrysalis
Of immortal love.

J.K. Ridley

About the Author

Sr. Anne Marie is a member of the Society of Our Lady of the Most Holy Trinity, an international missionary Society which is comprised of Priests, Religious Brothers and Sisters, and Laity, married and single, serving on Ecclesial Family Teams in areas of deepest need in 12 different countries around the world.

Sister is degreed in Early Childhood Education, studied Formation, Consecrated Life and Missiology at the Pontifical University Urbaniana in Rome, and has pursued training and formation in specialized areas including Theology of the Body, Women's issues in the Culture, Family Healing, Pro-Life ministries and ministry oriented to serving those with cancer or affected by the disease.

Sister has worked in mission in administration, education, the formation of sisters, seminarians, laity and in conducting retreats and days of recollection. She served as the SOLT General Sister Servant from 2003 to 2013, visiting and caring for the needs of the SOLT sisters all over the world.

She currently serves at Domus Trinitatis (Home of the Trinity) retreat and renewal center in Willey, Iowa. Sister writes regularly for the Catholic Globe of the Sioux City Diocese and various other Catholic publications.

She posts at: missionaryinthemodernworld.blogspot.com. Her other books: *Facing Our Immortality,* and *The Blessing Voice,* can be found on Amazon.

Made in the USA
Columbia, SC
28 March 2021